## To:

_____

## From:

_____

## Date:

_____

# DINOSAUR

## DEVOTIONS

75 Dino Discoveries,
Bible Truths, Fun Facts,
and More!

**MICHELLE MEDLOCK ADAMS**

ILLUSTRATED BY **DENISE TURU**

An Imprint of Thomas Nelson

## SPECIAL THANKS TO

**Wendy Lanier**, for being my buddy, brainstorming partner, occasional chauffeur, and dinosaur photographer as I worked on this dinosaur devotional. I appreciate you more than you know.

**Karissa Taylor**, my amazing editor who believed in this book from the very beginning and encouraged me every step of this Jurassic journey.

*Dinosaur Devotions*

© 2018 by Michelle Medlock Adams

Published in Nashville, Tennessee, by Tommy Nelson. Tommy Nelson is an imprint of Thomas Nelson. Thomas Nelson is a registered trademark of HarperCollins Christian Publishing, Inc.

Illustrated by Denise Turu.

Tommy Nelson titles may be purchased in bulk for educational, business, fund-raising, or sales promotional use. For information, please e-mail SpecialMarkets@ThomasNelson.com.

Scripture quotations marked CEV are taken from the Contemporary English Version. Copyright © 1991, 1992, 1995 by American Bible Society. Used by permission.

Scripture quotations marked ESV are taken from the ESV® Bible (The Holy Bible, English Standard Version®). Copyright © 2001 by Crossway, a publishing ministry of Good News Publishers. Used by permission. All rights reserved.

Scripture quotations marked MSG are taken from *The Message*. Copyright © by Eugene H. Peterson 1993, 1994, 1995, 1996, 2000, 2001, 2002. Used by permission of Tyndale House Publishers, Inc.

Scripture quotations marked NASB are taken from the New American Standard Bible®. Copyright © 1960, 1962, 1963, 1968, 1971, 1972, 1973, 1975, 1977, 1995 by The Lockman Foundation. Used by permission. (www.Lockman.org)

Scripture quotations marked NCV are taken from the New Century Version®. © 2005 by Thomas Nelson. Used by permission. All rights reserved.

Scripture quotations marked NIV are taken from the Holy Bible, New International Version®, NIV®. Copyright © 1973, 1978, 1984, 2011 by Biblica, Inc.® Used by permission of Zondervan. All rights reserved worldwide. www.zondervan.com. The "NIV" and "New International Version" are trademarks registered in the United States Patent and Trademark Office by Biblica, Inc.®

Scripture quotations marked NKJV are taken from the New King James Version®. © 1982 by Thomas Nelson. Used by permission. All rights reserved.

Scripture quotations marked NLT are taken from the Holy Bible, New Living Translation. © 1996, 2004, 2007, 2013 by Tyndale House Foundation. Used by permission of Tyndale House Publishers, Inc., Carol Stream, Illinois 60188. All rights reserved.

Scripture quotations marked TLB are taken from The Living Bible. Copyright © 1971. Used by permission of Tyndale House Publishers, Inc., Carol Stream, Illinois 60188. All rights reserved.

ISBN-13: 978-1-4002-0902-6

**Library of Congress Cataloging-in-Publication Data**

Names: Adams, Michelle Medlock, author.
Title: Dinosaur devotions : 75 dino discoveries, Bible truths, fun facts, and more! / Michelle Medlock Adams ; illustrated by Denise Turu.
Description: Nashville : Thomas Nelson, 2018. |
Identifiers: LCCN 2010001010 (print) | LCCN 2010035505 (ebook) | ISBN 9781400211043 (e-book) | ISBN 9781400209026 (hardcover)
Subjects: LCSH: Children--Religious life--Juvenile literature. | Devotional literature--Juvenile literature. | Dinosaurs--Miscellanea--Juvenile literature.
Classification: LCC BV4571.3 (ebook) | LCC BV4571.3 .A33 2018 (print) | DDC 242/.62--dc23
LC record available at https://lccn.loc.gov/2018021218

*Printed in China*
21 22 DSC 6 5 4 3

Mfr: DSC / Dongguan, China / September 2021 / PO #12102837

For Baby Bear.
Gigi loves you as big as a Patagotitan.

# CONTENTS

# UTAHRAPTOR
[YOO-tah-RAP-tor]

**BIBLE EXCAVATION:**

Together you are the body of Christ. Each one of you is part of his body.

—1 CORINTHIANS 12:27 CEV

## TEAM DINOSAUR

### DINO STATS

**FAMILY:**
Dromaeosauridae

**HEIGHT:**
6 ft. (1.8 m)
at the hip

**LENGTH:**
22 ft. (6.7 m)

**WEIGHT:**
1,500 lb. (680.4 kg)

**DIET:**
other dinosaurs

For a long time, the Utahraptor was almost unknown because no one had found many bones belonging to the large raptor. But in 2014, that all changed. Scientists discovered the bones of six Utahraptors on a mountain in the state of Utah. Finding so many Utahraptor skeletons together helped experts conclude that these dinosaurs probably stayed together and hunted in packs.

Have you ever heard the saying "Teamwork makes the dream work"? Well, in the Utahraptors' case, teamwork is how they filled their bellies. By working together to corner other dinosaurs, these raptors were able to hunt more effectively and feed every raptor in the pack.

You know, teamwork is important. Whether you're on a team trying to win a game or you're part of a group studying to get a good grade, working together to accomplish a common goal is a good idea. And it's not only a good idea. It's also a God idea!

God wants each of us to do what He has called us to do. He wants us to help Him share His love with the world. You might even say that we're on God's team, and that's a great team to be on.

## DIGGING DEEPER:

*As a part of God's team, what can you do to share His love with others?*

## JURASSIC JOURNALING:

*In your journal, write the letters T-E-A-M, and think of a word that begins with each letter and describes an aspect of being on a team. For example, for T you might write the word* together *because working together describes one important part of being on a team.*

 DID YOU KNOW . . . that the Utahraptor probably had feathers but wasn't able to fly?

# BRACHIOSAURUS
## [BRACK-ee-oh-SORE-us]

BIBLE EXCAVATION:

The Lord said to Samuel, "Don't judge by a man's face or height. . . .
I don't make decisions the way you do! Men judge by outward
appearance, but I look at a man's thoughts and intentions."

—1 SAMUEL 16:7 TLB

## DINO STATS

**FAMILY:**
Brachiosauridae

**HEIGHT:**
30 ft. (9.1 m)

**LENGTH:**
82 ft. (25 m)

**WEIGHT:**
40,000–100,000
lb. (18,143.7–
45,359.2 kg)

**DIET:**
plants

## LOOKS CAN BE DECEIVING

The Brachiosaurus is thought to be one of the largest land animals ever to have existed. But just because it was big doesn't mean it was ferocious. Scientists believe the Brachiosaurus was a gentle giant. It didn't even eat animals—it was strictly a plant-eater. Standing about 30 feet tall and weighing as much as 100,000 pounds, these dinosaurs probably looked pretty scary to most of the other dinosaurs. But they weren't much of a threat unless you were a tasty plant.

Many of the smaller meat-eating dinosaurs were fiercer than the Brachiosaurus. Still, as one of the biggest animals around, it probably intimidated everyone in its world—whether it meant to or not. Weighing about seven times more than a T. Rex, the Brachiosaurus likely made the ground shake with each step it took. When these large dinosaurs walked into an area to feed, other dinosaurs scattered.

In the case of the Brachiosaurus, looks can be deceiving. These gentle giants looked way scarier than

**DIGGING DEEPER:**

*Do you find it difficult to stop yourself from judging others? It can be a hard habit to break, but ask God. He will help you be less "judgey" and more accepting.*

**JURASSIC JOURNALING:**

*Write three things about yourself that people wouldn't know or even guess based on the way you look.*

they actually were. You might say they were misunderstood.

Have you ever felt misunderstood? Have you ever felt that people thought something about you based on your looks that simply wasn't true? Or have you ever misjudged someone based on his or her appearance? God wants us to follow His example and look beyond someone's exterior and focus on that person's heart. In other words, don't judge others before you get to know them. Just think, that really tall guy in your homeroom might just be a gentle giant. Why not give him a chance?

**DID YOU KNOW** . . . that *Brachiosaurus* means "arm reptiles"? The name refers to the dinosaur's huge front legs.

# TYRANNOSAURUS REX
## [tie-RAN-oh-SORE-us REX]

BIBLE EXCAVATION:

Don't you remember the rule we had when we lived with you? "If you don't work, you don't eat." And now we're getting reports that a bunch of lazy good-for-nothings are taking advantage of you. This must not be tolerated. We command them to get to work immediately—no excuses, no arguments—and earn their own keep. Friends, don't slack off in doing your duty.

—2 THESSALONIANS 3:10–13 MSG

## DON'T BE A LAZY LIZARD

### DINO STATS

**FAMILY:**
Tyrannosauridae

**HEIGHT:**
13 ft. (4 m)

**LENGTH:**
40 ft. (12.2 m)

**WEIGHT:**
14,000 lb.
(6,350.3 kg)

**DIET:**
other dinosaurs
(bones and all!)

Tyrannosaurus Rex is probably the most famous dinosaur of all, but it certainly wasn't the hardest working dino. In fact, as famous and ferocious as it has been portrayed in history, the T. Rex may have been kind of lazy. Some experts believe it ate injured, sickly, or dead animals so it didn't have to hunt. And when it did hunt, the T. Rex may have hidden behind trees and snuck up on unsuspecting plant-eating dinosaurs. In one short burst of energy, the T. Rex would grab its **prey** in its very powerful jaws and chomp away, using its six-inch-long fangs to easily break through bones.

You might say the T. Rex took the easiest route to a meal. Instead of hunting like many of the other meat-eating dinos, the T. Rex preferred to eat whatever was closest and easiest to conquer. Who would've dreamed that the T. Rex was a lazy lizard?

How about you? Are you ever a lazy lizard? Do you

DIGGING DEEPER:

In what area of your life are you being a lazy lizard? What changes can you make so that you honor God by doing your best?

JURASSIC JOURNALING:

Write two goals you have. It doesn't matter if they seem crazy—think big! Then write down the steps you need to take to accomplish those goals.

DINO DICTIONARY:

**prey**—a creature that is hunted and eaten by another animal.

sometimes take the easy way out, or do you work hard and do your best in every situation? Often the easiest way isn't the best way, and God has called us to be our best—every day in every way.

For example, if your mom tells you to clean up your room, you might be tempted to shove all the clutter under your bed so it's hidden when she does a room inspection. That's being a lazy lizard. A better way would be to put everything back in its place, creating a well-organized room. So don't be a lazy lizard. Honor God by doing your best at every task.

DID YOU KNOW . . . that the name *Tyrannosaurus Rex* means "king of the tyrant lizards"?

# IGUANODON
## [ig-WAH-na-DON]

**BIBLE EXCAVATION:**

"Seek first the kingdom of God and his righteousness, and all these things will be added to you."

—MATTHEW 6:33 ESV

## DINO STATS

**FAMILY:**
Iguanodontidae

**HEIGHT:**
16 ft. (4.9 m)

**LENGTH:**
33–39 ft.
(10.1–11.9 m)

**WEIGHT:**
10,000 lb.
(4,535.9 kg)

**DID YOU KNOW** . . . that scientists once thought Iguanodons were giant crocodiles?

**DIET:**
plants

# GET YOUR BALANCE

The Iguanodon had many unique features, such as a cone-shaped spike on its thumb that it may have used as a weapon against its enemies. It also had four other fingers on each of its hands so it could grab plants for an easy lunch. And though the Iguanodon usually walked on all four legs, it was able to run on its big back legs while keeping its body in a horizontal position. Its stiff, heavy tail helped the large dinosaur balance itself. Without that tail, the Iguanodon probably would have toppled if it tried to run on two legs. Its tail was the key to balancing its large body.

How is your balance? Have you ever tried to stand on one leg and then extend the other leg behind you without toppling over? Try it. It's not easy!

Being off balance isn't good in any area of life. For example, if you're so busy with sports, homework, and playing video games that you have no time to spend with God, then you're off balance. You might fall on your face! So ask God to be your "tail" and help you keep your life balanced. When you put God first in your life, He will help you do everything you need to do. He wants to be involved in every part of your life. And when you involve Him, He will help keep your life in perfect balance.

### DIGGING DEEPER:

*When was the last time you took time to pray to God or read the Bible? Are you too busy for Him? What activity can you cut back on so you have time to spend with God?*

### JURASSIC JOURNALING:

*Write your to-do list for the day, and then ask God to help you get everything done on your list. Start doing this every day!*

# KENTROSAURUS
## [KEN-troh-SORE-us]

**BIBLE EXCAVATION:**

I praise you because I am fearfully and wonderfully made.

—PSALM 139:14 NIV

## DINO STATS

**FAMILY:**
Stegosauridae

**HEIGHT:**
6–11.5 ft. (1.8–3.5 m)

**LENGTH:**
15–17 ft. (4.6–5.2 m)

**WEIGHT:**
2,000–4,000 lb.
(907.2–1,814.4 kg)

**DIET:**
plants

## YOU'RE SPECIAL

The Kentrosaurus, a type of Stegosaur, had a very small head and a tiny brain no bigger than a walnut. But what it lacked in smarts the Kentrosaurus made up for with a double row of spikes down its back from its midsection to its tail. This dinosaur would use its plated tail to ward off meat-eating dinosaurs. Those rows of long, sharp spikes were frightening enough to scare off its enemies.

So even though the Kentrosaurus didn't have the brains to figure out how to escape its enemies, it had a built-in weapon on its back to defend itself. That made this dinosaur very unique and special. It had just what it needed to survive.

God made you very special too. Even if you're not the smartest, fastest, or tallest in your family, you have qualities that make you extra special. God made each

**DID YOU KNOW . . .** that *Kentrosaurus* actually means "spiky lizard"?

of us for a specific purpose, and each of us has just what we need to not only survive but thrive. So don't worry if you're not the smartest or fastest or tallest or strongest. You are a one-of-a-kind masterpiece, and you're exactly who God created you to be. In fact, the Bible says you are fearfully and wonderfully made. God took great care when making you, and you can be sure that God doesn't make mistakes. You are special!

# EDMONTONIA
## [ED-mon-TONE-ee-ah]

**BIBLE EXCAVATION:**

Be strong in the Lord and in his mighty power. Put on the full armor of God, so that you can take your stand against the devil's schemes.

—EPHESIANS 6:10-11 NIV

## DINO STATS

**FAMILY:**
Nodosauridae

**HEIGHT:**
6 ft. (1.8 m)

**LENGTH:**
22–23 ft. (6.7–7 m)

**WEIGHT:**
8,000 lb. (3,628.7 kg)

**DIET:**
plants

 **DID YOU KNOW . . .** that Edmonton, a city in Canada, is one of the few regions in the world with two dinosaurs named after it? (The duck-billed Edmontosaurus and the armored Edmontonia.)

# WHERE'S YOUR ARMOR?

The Edmontonia was a bulky, armored, tank-like dinosaur. It was covered in bony plates, and along its sides were large spikes. This dangerous dino also sported a seriously scary set of shoulder pads, with some of its shoulder spikes reaching over a foot long!

All this "hardware" was a great security feature. It not only looked scary, but it was also much harder for a meat-eating dino to devour. ("I'll have the Edmontonia. Hold the spikes and armor, please.") Plus, it could charge at its enemies and use its shoulder spikes as weapons, or it could whip its bony-plated tail at its enemies and do some major damage. You might say the Edmontonia was armed and dangerous.

Did you know that as a child of God, you also have armor available to you? The armor of God! Okay, it may not include foot-long spikes on your shoulders, but it's pretty impressive. It includes the belt of truth, the breastplate of righteousness, the shoes of the gospel of peace, the shield of faith, the helmet of salvation, and the sword of the Spirit. Of course, you can't see your armor—it's invisible. But that doesn't make it any less powerful.

Just as the Edmontonia had enemies in the animal kingdom, we also have an enemy—the Devil. God has given us this special armor to use against that enemy. All we have to do is put it on, and we do that by praying, worshipping, and reading the Bible. So put that armor on today and every day! You'll be armed and equipped for the kingdom of God.

**DIGGING DEEPER:**

*As one of God's warriors, how can you use each piece of spiritual armor every day?*

**JURASSIC JOURNALING:**

*Write the name of each piece of spiritual armor. Writing them out will help you memorize them so you can mentally and spiritually put on each piece every day.*

# DIMETRODON
## [die-MET-roe-DON]

## STEP INTO THE LIGHT

### DINO STATS

**FAMILY:**
Sphenacodontidae

**HEIGHT:**
3 ft. (0.9 m)

**LENGTH:**
10–15 ft. (3–4.6 m)

**WEIGHT:**
60–500 lb.
(27.2–226.8 kg)

**DIET:**
other animals

Okay, so the Dimetrodon wasn't *actually* a dinosaur, though many have mistaken it for one. In reality, it was a reptile-looking, mammal-like creature that had many dinosaur characteristics. The Dimetrodon is sort of a *nondinosaur* dinosaur.

This creature was quite unique in the looks department. It had a large sail that covered its back and wasn't just for decoration. Scientists believe this sail, which stood as high as three feet tall, served as a giant temperature gauge. Since the Dimetrodon was probably cold-blooded, scientists think this nondinosaur would stand with its sail facing the sun during the day to soak up warmth. At night the built-up heat would help keep the Dimetrodon's body temperature stable. The Dimetrodon had a built-in thermostat. Pretty cool, huh?

Just like the Dimetrodon had to bask in the sun every day, we need to soak up a different type of *sun*—the Son of God. The Son's presence warms us up from the inside out. In other words, we need to spend time with the Lord

## DIGGING DEEPER:

*How has spending time with God affected your attitude?*

## JURASSIC JOURNALING:

*Sometimes it's hard to find time to "bask in the Son." So make a list of your daily activities and see what time you have available to spend with Him. A great option is to spend time with God as soon as you wake up.*

every single day to keep us stable. When you read the Bible and pray, you will be stable in any situation—even when your sibling picks a fight and gets you in trouble with your parents. So take a lesson from the Dimetrodon—bask in the Son.

 DID YOU KNOW . . . that the name *Dimetrodon* means "two-measures of teeth," meaning it had two different kinds of teeth?

# MICROPACHYCEPHALOSAURUS
[MY-cro-PACK-ee-SEFF-ah-low-SORE-us]

**BIBLE EXCAVATION:**

Thus says the LORD, he who created you, O Jacob, he who formed you, O Israel: "Fear not, for I have redeemed you; I have called you by name, you are mine."

—ISAIAH 43:1 ESV

## DINO STATS

**FAMILY:**
Pachycephalosauridae

**HEIGHT:**
1–3 ft. (0.3–0.9 m)

**LENGTH:**
1–4 ft. (0.3–1.2 m)

**WEIGHT:**
5–10 lb. (2.3–4.5 kg)

**DIET:**
plants

## WHAT'S IN A NAME?

I'm pretty sure that if we'd been friends with the Micropachycephalosaurus, we would've given it a nickname—maybe Micro? Yes, let's call it Micro. Because a nine-syllable, twenty-three-letter name is a mouthful! In fact, this dinosaur holds the record for the longest name, yet it was one of the smallest dinosaurs. *Micropachycephalosaurus* actually means "small, thick-headed lizard." (Not sure that's any better than the nine-syllable mega-name!)

Names are important because they mean something. For instance, my name is *Michelle*, which means "godly woman." I may not always live up to that name, but every time someone says my name, they are saying, "Hello there, godly woman. How's it going today, godly woman? Would you pass me the ketchup, godly woman?" Pretty cool, huh? Even if your name doesn't mean something like "godly girl" or "godly guy," if you are a Christ follower, you are called a *Christian*. That means you have part of Christ's name in *your* name! And that's really awesome!

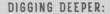

DIGGING DEEPER:

*If you could make up a name for God, what would it be? Here's a helpful hint: base your name for God on something that He's done for you or on what He means to you.*

JURASSIC JOURNALING:

*Ask your parents if they know the meaning of your name. If they don't, go to your local library and find a book of baby names to find the meaning of your name, and write it in your journal.*

God has many names too, and they all mean something different. Each name of God shows a characteristic of His nature. For instance, *Jehovah Jireh* means "the God who provides." And *Jehovah-shalom* means "the God of peace."

No matter what your name means (hopefully it doesn't mean "small, thick-headed lizard"), you can celebrate that God knows your name. You're a child of God. And that means you are awesome, chosen, and loved.

**DID YOU KNOW** . . . that before the Micropachycephalosaurus was discovered, the Compsognathus was the smallest dinosaur ever found?

23

# STYRACOSAURUS
## [sty-RACK-oh-SORE-us]

All Scripture is breathed out by God and profitable for teaching, for reproof, for correction, and for training in righteousness.

—2 TIMOTHY 3:16 ESV

## GO TO THE SOURCE

**DINO STATS**

**FAMILY:**
Ceratopsidae

**HEIGHT:**
6 ft. (1.8 m)

**LENGTH:**
16–18 ft.
(4.9–5.5 m)

**WEIGHT:**
6,000 lb.
(2,721.6 kg)

**DIET:**
plants

The Styracosaurus had one of the scariest, most intimidating heads of any dinosaur. With horns and spikes on its nose and the back of its neck, the Styracosaurus might appear to be a ferocious, meat-eating dino. But it actually ate only plants. In fact, most dinosaurs were vegetarians. You might have thought all dinosaurs were fierce hunters, but most were content to chew on stalks and plants.

Just because you've heard something or seen something many times, that doesn't necessarily make it true. You have to go to a reliable source to get the facts. This is true whether you're talking about dinosaurs, the weather forecast, or God. You can't always trust what others tell you, and you can't believe everything you read on the Internet. You need to find out for yourself. For example, to learn more details about this dinosaur, I had to rely on information from scientists specializing in the study of dinosaurs. I couldn't just watch a few dinosaur movies and write about dinosaurs based on what I saw. I had to go to a trustworthy source.

DIGGING DEEPER:

*Have you ever believed something to be true only to learn later you were misinformed? How did you feel when you found out the truth?*

JURASSIC JOURNALING:

*Do you want to use a reliable source to learn more about what God's like? Grab your Bible and read Exodus 34:6. Write down your favorite fact about God from this verse.*

This is especially true when it comes to God. Don't go by what the world tells you about God, because the world rarely gets it right. Go to the Word of God and find out what the Bible says about Him. And read it regularly because God will reveal new truths about Himself to you as you study His Word.

Who wants secondhand information when you can get the truth by going to the real source?

DID YOU KNOW . . . that the Styracosaurus was covered in a super thick hide?

# PARASAUROLOPHUS
[par-ah-SORE-OL-uh-fus]

Shout for joy to the LORD, all the earth, burst into jubilant song with music.

—PSALM 98:4 NIV

## DINO STATS

**FAMILY:**
Hadrosauridae

**HEIGHT:**
16 ft. (4.9 m)

**LENGTH:**
35 ft. (10.7 m)

**WEIGHT:**
6,000–8,000
lb. (2,721.6–
3,628.7 kg)

**DIET:**
plants

DID YOU KNOW . . . that as the
Parasaurolophus's teeth wore down in the front
of its mouth, new teeth moved forward, a process
that continued throughout this dino's life?

# MAKE A JOYFUL NOISE

The Parasaurolophus was quite an odd-looking dinosaur. It was a member of the Hadrosaurs, but most just call this dino group the "duck-bills" because of their duck-like appearance. And there's more—this dinosaur had a hollow tube-like crest on its head that reached up to six feet long! One **paleontologist** believed the crest contained scent glands or possibly helped the dino breathe underwater. Others disagree. But most agree that this crest served the Parasaurolophus as a noisemaker. In fact, it made a sound sort of like a trumpet! Some experts say the crest made a low B-flat note, like an elephant's trumpet, and that's how the dinosaur communicated with other dinos.

It's pretty cool that the Parasaurolophus had its own built-in musical instrument. And while we may not have a trumpet growing out of our heads, we can still make a joyful noise to the Lord. We can use our hands to clap and our voices to sing. Even if you don't think you have a beautiful singing voice, God still loves to hear your songs of praise. And you don't have to know any worship songs—you can just make up your own!

Singing to God not only pleases our heavenly Father, but it also strengthens us and makes us more joyful. And it's contagious—those who hear our joyful noise will be encouraged and filled with joy. It's a win-win situation. So go ahead. Make a joyful noise!

**DIGGING DEEPER:**

*How does it make you feel when you sing to the Lord? You don't have to be loud or even sing really well. He still loves to hear your songs of praise.*

**JURASSIC JOURNALING:**

*Write the letters P-R-A-I-S-E down the side of a piece of paper, and then write something you're thankful for that begins with each letter.*

**DINO DICTIONARY:**

***paleontologist***—*a scientist who studies animals that no longer exist (like dinosaurs), their environments, and their behavior.*

# ANKYLOSAURUS
## [AN-kye-loh-SORE-us]

**BIBLE EXCAVATION:**

We have everything we need to live a life that pleases God.
It was all given to us by God's own power, when we learned that
he had invited us to share in his wonderful goodness.

—2 PETER 1:3 CEV

## DINO STATS

**FAMILY:**
Ankylosauridae

**HEIGHT:**
5–6 ft. (1.5–1.8 m)

**LENGTH:**
20–23 ft. (6.1–7 m)

**WEIGHT:**
8,800–15,000
lb. (3,991.6–
6,803.9 kg)

**DIET:**
plants

## YOU'VE GOT ALL YOU NEED

The Ankylosaurus was one of the largest armor-plated dinos to ever walk the earth. Because of its weight and size, Anky not only looked like a tank; it also moved as slow as one. And since it existed at the same time as the T. Rex and other meat-eating dinosaurs, the slow-moving Anky was an easy target for a meal. But luckily, it had other defenses.

This dinosaur had extremely tough, leathery skin. Plus, it had two rows of spikes down its back, large horns on top of its head, and a spikey, club-like tail. All this made old Anky a less-than-tasty meal option for the hungry, meat-eating dinosaurs. Imagine the steak you ordered was brought to you covered in leather with nails piled on top. I'm guessing you'd push your plate away and order something else. That's exactly what the T. Rex and other meat-eating dinos did. They opted for more

DID YOU KNOW . . . that although the Ankylosaurus
was quite large, it had tiny teeth?

*Old Anky had heavy armor that made him slow but also made him an unappealing snack to other dinos. Is there something about you that might seem like a negative, yet God uses it in your life as a positive?*

## JURASSIC JOURNALING:

*Describe a time when you didn't think you had everything you needed to succeed, but in the end, you actually did!*

## DINO DICTIONARY:

**predator**—*an animal that hunts and kills other animals for food.*

appealing, easier-to-eat dinosaurs. So even though the Ankylosaurus was easy to catch, its tough skin and armor were just what it needed to protect itself from **predators**.

God will give you exactly what you need too. For example, when you're feeling sad, you can ask Him to fill you up with His joy. And when you're feeling scared, you can pray to God and thank Him that He is always with you. God knows what we need before we need it because He can see the beginning to the end and everything in between. So don't worry that you are lacking in any way. You have everything you'll ever need to survive and thrive.

# PTEROSAUR
## [TER-uh-SORE]

It's healthy to be content, but envy can eat you up.

—PROVERBS 14:30 CEV

## DINO STATS

**FAMILY:**
Archosaurs

**HEIGHT:**
up to 18 ft. (5.5 m)

**WINGSPAN:**
10 in.–30 ft. (0.3–9.1 m)

**WEIGHT:**
up to 550 lb. (249.5 kg)

**DIET:**
fish, insects, small
land animals

## NO MORE GREEN-EYED MONSTER

The Pterosaurs weren't exactly dinosaurs. These beaked reptiles were cousins of the dinosaurs. Few Pterosaur **fossils** have been recovered, so we don't know much about them. But we do know they were flying reptiles, and some were quite large with a 30-foot wingspan! Experts believe they were one of the only reptiles to ever fly. They were also the biggest flying animals to have ever lived!

Their "claim to fame" is pretty amazing. So amazing, in fact, that their uniqueness and abilities would probably make even the most famous dinosaurs a little jealous—especially if they needed to escape from a predator.

Have you ever felt jealous of a friend, a sibling, or a cousin? It happens. You may feel pretty good about your basketball skills until your brother sinks ten three-pointers in a row. Or you may be happy about your grades until you find out your best friend has the highest grade point average in your entire class. That's when a different kind of creature rears its ugly head—the green-eyed monster! That's what some people call jealousy, and it is an ugly animal. The Bible says that where you find jealousy and selfishness, you will find every evil thing (James 3:16). Yikes! That green-eyed monster is way scarier than any dinosaur!

To keep jealousy out of your life, stop comparing yourself to others and start thinking about how awesome God is. Remember the special abilities and characteristics He has given you, and celebrate those things!

DID YOU KNOW . . . that the name *Pterosaur* is Greek for "wing lizards"?

**DIGGING DEEPER:**

*When was the last time you felt jealous? How did you get over those feelings?*

**JURASSIC JOURNALING:**

*Write the names of the people you are most jealous of, and now make that your new prayer list. It's hard to be jealous of someone and pray for that person at the same time.*

**DINO DICTIONARY:**

**fossil**—*a trace element of an ancient animal or plant, such as an impression in a rock, a preserved body part, a footprint, or a bone.*

# BAROSAURUS
## [BAR-oh-SORE-us]

BIBLE EXCAVATION:

We know that in all things God works for the good of those who love him, who have been called according to his purpose.

—ROMANS 8:28 NIV

## GOD CAN USE IT

### DINO STATS

**FAMILY:**
Diplodocidae

**HEIGHT:**
40 ft. (12.2 m)

**LENGTH:**
79–89 ft.
(24.1–27.1 m)

**WEIGHT:**
50,000 lb.
(22,679.6 kg)

**DIET:**
plants

The Barosaurus was a long dinosaur with a long neck, perfect for reaching leaves in surrounding trees without ever having to move. Like many plant-eating dinosaurs, the Barosaurus swallowed tough leaves and twigs whole. It didn't even chew! (Can you imagine swallowing a cheeseburger without taking a bite?) And as it devoured plants and twigs, it swallowed rocks too.

*Rocks?* You're probably thinking this dino got some bad tummy aches, right? But surprisingly, these rocks were good for the Barosaurus! Because these dinosaurs swallowed their food whole, they needed the rocks to help break down the food so it could be properly digested. Swallowing rocks served an important purpose in the Barosaurus's life.

You know, that's true in our lives too. Occasionally, something that seems bad at first turns out to be good for us. What looks like a negative can actually have a positive impact. For example, finding out you're not in your

**DIGGING DEEPER:**

*Think of a time when something bad happened in your life and God used that situation for good.*

**JURASSIC JOURNALING:**

*Write about something negative in your life right now, and leave a spot below for an update. Then when something positive comes from that negative situation, update your journal entry.*

best friend's class can seem like a bad thing. But being in a different class leads you to make new friends you wouldn't have made. Now you have several friends in your new class. So what looked like a bad situation actually produced a good thing in your life—more friends!

Do your best to find something positive from each negative situation. And ask God to help you. He will because He rocks—way more than the rocks in the belly of the Barosaurus.

**DID YOU KNOW** . . . that a Barosaurus could hold its head up to about 50 feet above the ground?

# OVIRAPTOR
## [OH-vih-RAP-tore]

**BIBLE EXCAVATION:**

If we confess our sins to God, he can always be trusted to forgive us and take our sins away.

—1 JOHN 1:9 CEV

## WHAT'S IN A NAME?

### DINO STATS

**FAMILY:**
Oviraptoridae

**HEIGHT:**
3–5 ft. (0.9–1.5 m)

**LENGTH:**
8 ft. (2.4 m)

**WEIGHT:**
45 lb. (20.4 kg)

**DIET:**
reptiles, nuts, fruits

The Oviraptor was a bird-like dino. According to experts, it was most likely feathered and had a beaked jaw instead of teeth. Its jaws were thought to be powerful enough to crush shellfish and eggs. Speaking of eggs, *Oviraptor* actually means "egg thief." Explorer Roy Chapman Andrews named this dino because its bones were found near a nest of eggs. The Oviraptor's skull had been crushed, so Andrews thought it was killed while trying to steal eggs from another dinosaur. This turned out not to be true, but Roy had already named it "egg thief."

Can you imagine being named after something bad you'd done (or hadn't done, as in the Oviraptor's case) or some failure you'd had? Instead of being named *Wesley* or *Ally*, you might be named *Yelled at My Sister* or *Failed My Math Test*. You would be reminded of that mistake every time someone called your name.

In the Bible God changed people's names when they had a change of heart or direction. For instance, He renamed *Sarai* (which means "my princess") to *Sarah*

**DIGGING DEEPER:**

*Have you ever wanted to change your name? What name would you choose and why?*

**JURASSIC JOURNALING:**

*Write about a time you were accused of something you didn't do. How did that make you feel?*

(which means "mother of nations") once she became pregnant with Isaac. He changed *Jacob* (which means "the deceiver") to *Israel* (which means "he wrestles with God").

Have you had a change of heart or direction in your life? Even if your name doesn't change, your heart can. God promises to forgive us if we confess our sins and ask for forgiveness. So just ask Him. Who needs a new name if you have a brand-new heart?

**DID YOU KNOW . . .** that a second Oviraptor skeleton was discovered on top of its nest of eggs? A sandstorm or a collapsing sand dune likely killed that Oviraptor as it sat on its eggs. It died being a good parent, not an egg thief. Many experts think the Oviraptor was misnamed and that the first dino that was found wasn't trying to steal those eggs but rather to protect them.

# APATOSAURUS
## [uh-PAT-uh-SORE-us]

BIBLE EXCAVATION:

GOD guards you from every evil, he guards your very life.

—PSALM 121:7 MSG

## FIERCE LOVE

### DINO STATS

**FAMILY:**
Diplodocidae

**HEIGHT:**
30 ft. (9.1 m)

**LENGTH:**
69–90 ft.
(21–27.4 m)

**WEIGHT:**
40,000–72,000
lb. (18,143.7–
32,658.7 kg)

**DIET:**
plants

The Apatosaurus was one big dino! In fact, an average adult Apatosaurus was longer than two school buses, was as tall as a full-grown dogwood tree, and weighed as much as six elephants!

The Apatosaurus was not only huge, but it was also hugely protective—especially when it came to its young. This massive dinosaur laid eggs and carefully guarded those eggs until they hatched. To protect its babies, experts believe this dino would rear up on its hind legs and whip its tail back and forth to ward off attackers. Adult Apatosauruses would also keep their young in the center of their pack to hide them from nearby predators.

Parents are known to be very protective of their children—whether we're talking about dinosaurs or humans. It's a natural instinct for parents to protect their babies. That's why your parents may get really upset when they find out somebody is being mean to you. They can't help themselves. They love you that much,

DIGGING DEEPER:

*Why do you think
God is so protective
of you? How does
that make you feel?*

JURASSIC
JOURNALING:

*Write a thank-you note
to your parents for loving
you and protecting you.
Let them know how much
you appreciate their
fierce love.*

and they want to protect you from all physical and mental harm. God is the same way—He is the ultimate protective parent. The Bible says He covers us like a bird protects her babies with her wings. The Bible also says that He will never leave us. Your heavenly Father's love for you is bigger than an Apatosaurus, and that's a lot!

DID YOU KNOW . . . that the name *Apatosaurus* means "deceptive lizard"? Scientists chose this name because its bones looked so much like several other dinosaurs.

# STEGOSAURUS
## [STEG-oh-SORE-us]

BIBLE EXCAVATION:

The LORD grants wisdom! From his mouth come knowledge and understanding. He grants a treasure of common sense to the honest. He is a shield to those who walk with integrity.

—PROVERBS 2:6–7 NLT

## DINO STATS

**FAMILY:**
Stegosauridae

**HEIGHT:**
9 ft. (2.7 m)

**LENGTH:**
26–30 ft.
(7.9–9.1 m)

**WEIGHT:**
6,800 lb.
(3,084.4 kg)

**DIET:**
plants

# IF I ONLY HAD A BRAIN . . . OR TWO

The Stegosaurus was an impressive-looking dinosaur. It had large, upright plates down its back, and at the very tip of its tail were several long spikes—perfect for intimidating its enemies. Scientists believe the Stegosaurus would swing its tail from side to side with great power and use it as a weapon against predators.

But as big and powerful as the Stegosaurus was, its brain was the size of a walnut. Scientists couldn't figure out how a dinosaur so large could survive with a brain so small. In fact, at one point, some experts thought the Stegosaurus had two brains.

Can you imagine having two brains? Wouldn't that be amazing? If you had two brains working for you, I bet you'd probably know exactly what to do in every situation. And you'd be able to come up with witty ideas and inventions that would change the world!

Well, you may not have two brains, but you have something even better—you have a very wise heavenly Father. The Bible says, "If you need wisdom, ask our generous God, and he will give it to you" (James 1:5 NLT). We don't need two brains to do great things. We just need God.

**DIGGING DEEPER:**

*Where do you go when you need wise advice—the Bible, your parents, a teacher, your best friend?*

**JURASSIC JOURNALING:**

*Think of a situation in your life where you could use a little wisdom. Write a prayer to God asking for His wisdom and help.*

**DID YOU KNOW** . . . that scientists later discovered that the Stegosaurus's "second brain" was actually just a nerve center that controlled the dino's back legs and tail?

# YUTYRANNUS
## [YOO-tie-RAN-us]

"I know the plans I have for you," declares the LORD, "plans to prosper you and not to harm you, plans to give you hope and a future."

—JEREMIAH 29:11 NIV

### DINO STATS

**FAMILY:**
Tyrannosauridae

**HEIGHT:**
9 ft. (2.7 m)

**LENGTH:**
30 ft. (9.1 m)

**WEIGHT:**
3,100 lb.
(1,406.1 kg)

**DIET:**
other animals

## GOD HAS A PLAN

The Yutyrannus was in the same family as the Tyrannosaurus Rex, but a special feature made it stand out: feathers. The Yutyrannus is the biggest feathered dinosaur we know of, and it's the largest feathered animal to have lived. Most animals as large as the Yutyrannus are hairless and featherless, but scientists believe that this dino grew feathers to keep warm, which means they were most likely warm-blooded like us. The Yutyrannus likely needed its feathers for insulation because it lived in colder climates.

God always knows what we need before we ever need it. (If you'd needed feathers, you'd have them!) You know, sometimes we don't understand why we are the way we are, but later we find out that God had a reason. He made us exactly the way we are because He has a plan for each one of our lives. For example, you may

DID YOU KNOW . . . that the name *Yutyrannus* means "feathered tyrant"?

## DIGGING DEEPER:

*What plans do you think God has for you? Do you feel like you have everything you need to fulfill those plans?*

## JURASSIC JOURNALING:

*What are two things you're good at or make you unique? Now write a way that God might use those unique qualities.*

be the comic of the family—the one who makes everyone laugh on long car rides. You think it's no big deal, but God may have created you to be funny so that you can be a Christian comic and tour the world, sharing about God through making people laugh. You just never know what God has planned, but *He* knows, and all you have to do is follow Him and trust that He made you exactly the way you are for a reason.

Whatever God has called you to do or wherever He has called you to go, isn't it comforting to know He has already equipped you for it? With or without feathers, God has given you wings to fly. So spread those wings!

# GIGANOTOSAURUS
## [JIG-ah-NOT-oh-SORE-us]

## DINO STATS

**FAMILY:**
Carcharodontosauridae

**HEIGHT:**
12 ft. (3.7 m) at the hips

**LENGTH:**
46 ft. (14 m)

**WEIGHT:**
18,000 lb. (8,164.7 kg)

**DIET:**
large plant-eating dinosaurs

DID YOU KNOW . . . that the Giganotosaurus had a brain half the size of its cousin the Tyrannosaurus Rex's brain?

# BE THE BEST YOU!

One day a mechanic riding on a dune buggy discovered the remains of a Giganotosaurus in the Argentine desert, and it was big news! Up until that time, the Tyrannosaurus Rex was thought to be the biggest meat-eating dinosaur. But the length of the Giganotosaurus was estimated to be 46 feet—that's six feet longer than the T. Rex!

And just when everyone thought that the Giganotosaurus was the biggest meat-eating dinosaur of all time, paleontologists found the remains of the Spinosaurus. And just like that, the Giganotosaurus was no longer the biggest meat-eating dinosaur of all time. It had been dethroned by the Spinosaurus, which scientists estimated to be 59 feet long. And recently the Patagotitan was declared the biggest dinosaur ever (though it was thought to be a plant-eater, not a meat-eater like the others), with a length of 122 feet from nose to tail.

You know, that's just how life goes. No matter how big, strong, fierce, smart, or fast you are, there will always be someone bigger, stronger, fiercer, smarter, and faster. And that's okay because you aren't competing with everyone else. You just need to be the best that you can be. Don't be discouraged when others are better than you at something. Instead, be confident in who God made you to be, and ask Him to help you be the very best version of you.

DIGGING DEEPER:

*How can you be a better version of you?*

JURASSIC JOURNALING:

*Write a short rhyme about being the best you that you can be.*

# VELOCIRAPTOR
## [veh-LOSS-ih-RAP-tore]

Be on your guard; stand firm in the faith; be courageous; be strong.

—1 CORINTHIANS 16:13 NIV

## SMALL BUT FEARLESS!

**DINO STATS**

**FAMILY:**
Dromaeosauridae

**HEIGHT:**
3 ft. (0.9 m)
at the hips

**LENGTH:**
6 ft. (1.8 m)

**WEIGHT:**
15–33 lb. (6.8–15 kg)

**DIET:**
small lizards, other
dinosaurs, eggs

Even if you're not a dinosaur expert, you may recognize the Velociraptor. The Velociraptors were big stars in some popular dinosaur movies. However, in real life, they were much smaller than they appeared in the movies. In fact, experts have estimated that most Velociraptors were about the size of a turkey. But even though they were small, they were mighty. They would attack dinosaurs that were bigger (even ones with big horns and claws) and fight to the death. In other words, the Velociraptor wouldn't back down—ever!

While we shouldn't be vicious like the Velociraptor, we can learn from its fearlessness. We don't have to let our size—no matter how small we may feel—keep us from doing what's right, even if it's scary. In the Bible, David was the youngest in his family, yet God called him to defeat the giant Goliath! It seems God should've called one of David's older, bigger brothers, but He didn't. And the best part? David didn't back down, and he defeated Goliath! David wasn't afraid, because he knew God was with him and had prepared him for that important battle.

## DIGGING DEEPER:

*What are you afraid of today? Do you ever feel scared or intimidated because of your age or size?*

## JURASSIC JOURNALING:

*Write some of your biggest fears—especially when it comes to following God. For example, are you afraid to follow God's plan for your life because He might call you to be a missionary in a foreign land? C'mon, be honest. Write them down. Now write these words over the top of your fears: "NO FEAR HERE!"*

So what are you afraid of today? What's keeping you from following God's plan for your life? You don't have to be scared when you're walking with God. He will go with you every step of the way. So be like the Velociraptor and David. Be fearless and have faith in God, knowing you're ready for any battle that comes your way.

**DID YOU KNOW** . . . that the name *Velociraptor* means "speedy thief"?

# PACHYCEPHALOSAURUS
## [pack-ih-SEFF-ah-low-SORE-us]

**BIBLE EXCAVATION:**

You made them only a little lower than God
and crowned them with glory and honor.

—PSALM 8:5 NLT

## PUT ON THAT CROWN

### DINO STATS

**FAMILY:**
Pachycephalosauridae

**HEIGHT:**
17–18 ft. (5.2–5.5 m)

**LENGTH:**
15 ft. (4.6 m)

**WEIGHT:**
1,000–2,200 lb.
(453.6–997.9 kg)

**DIET:**
plants and insects

**N**ot a lot is known about the Pachycephalosaurus because only one close-to-complete skull has been found. But one thing is for sure: this dino had a large skull with a large skull plate, which protected its small brain. Paleontologists believe that its thick skull—which was nearly 10 inches thick—was used as a weapon against its enemies. Some believe this dinosaur head-butted its enemies with its crown of spikes.

Did you know that you have something in common with a Pachycephalosaurus? It's true! You also have a crown. Okay, maybe it's not a crown of spikes, but it's definitely a crown. According to the Bible, as Christians, we are crowned with glory and honor. Pretty cool, huh? Think of it this way. God is your heavenly Father, and He is the King of kings. As his daughter or son, you are a princess or a prince, so that means you are royalty. And what do royals wear? They wear crowns. Now, you might not be able to see your crown, but just know that it's there. When you know you're wearing a crown, when

DIGGING DEEPER:

*How would you act differently if your dad was royalty? Well, your heavenly Father is!*

JURASSIC JOURNALING:

*Write five things that you associate with royalty.*

you know that your Father is the King of kings, when you know you are royalty . . . you will stand a little taller, walk a little more confidently, and be ready to face any challenge.

So wear that invisible crown every single day. It's *way* better than the Pachycephalosaurus's crown of spikes.

**DID YOU KNOW** . . . that some paleontologists think the Pachycephalosaurus resembled an armadillo?

# GIRAFFATITAN
## [jih-RAFF-ah-TIE-tan]

## DINO STATS

**FAMILY:**
Brachiosauridae

**HEIGHT:**
39–49 ft.
(11.9–14.9 m)

**LENGTH:**
72–85 ft.
(21.9–25.9 m)

**WEIGHT:**
51,000–87,000 lb. (23,133.2–39,462.5 kg)

**DIET:**
plants

## YOU'RE AN ORIGINAL

Because the Giraffatitan has a giraffe-like build, this dinosaur's name is spot on. For many years, the Giraffatitan was thought to be the largest dinosaur, but several other larger dinosaur fossils have since been found. Still, it was quite massive. When the Giraffatitan was first discovered, the paleontologists thought it was a Brachiosaurus because they looked so much alike. In fact, experts argued about this issue for many years. But in 2009 a man named Michael Taylor studied the differences between the Giraffatitan and the Brachiosaurus, and he proved that the Giraffatitan was a different dino and deserved its own name.

Aren't you glad that you haven't had to prove you deserve your own name? That you're an original? Even if you're an identical twin, you are still different than your sibling. For example, your fingerprints are not the same, and you probably have very different hopes and dreams.

Have you ever wondered why you were created or what God has planned for your life? If you ask God to show you, He will. Just keep trusting Him.

What are some physical qualities that make you different than your family? For example, do you have blonde hair and your brother has red hair? What things do you have in common with your family? Make a list of both your differences and the things you have in common.

God made you unique. There's only one you, and that means no one else looks exactly like you, shares the exact same dreams, or has your exact same abilities. That's why the Bible tells us that we are God's handiwork. God created you, and He doesn't make copies. He only makes originals, and you, my friend, are a masterpiece.

DID YOU KNOW . . . that the name *Giraffatitan* means "giant giraffe"?

# TROODON
## [TRO-oh-don]

I pray that the eyes of your heart may be enlightened in order
that you may know the hope to which he has called you.

—EPHESIANS 1:18 NIV

## DINO STATS

**FAMILY:**
Troodontidae

**HEIGHT:**
3 ft. (0.9 m)

**LENGTH:**
6–13 ft. (1.8–4 m)

**WEIGHT:**
110 lb. (49.9 kg)

**DIET:**
small animals

**DID YOU KNOW** . . . that the Troodon's
eyes were set toward the front of its
face, giving it advanced binocular vision?

# NIGHT VISION

When paleontologist Joseph Leidy examined the first fossil of the Troodon—which was only one tooth—he thought it was a lizard. It wasn't until later he realized it was a dinosaur, and not just any dinosaur. Some scientists believe the Troodon was the smartest dinosaur that ever lived. Its brain was six times heavier than other dinos its same size. It also had great hearing and large eyes that enabled the Troodon to see very well at night. In fact, experts believe it hunted at night because it gave this dino an advantage over all the animals who were sure to become the Troodon's dinner.

Have you ever worn night-vision goggles? They're really cool because they help you see clearly at night—probably similar to how the Troodon saw at night. Well, guess what! We can see things clearly, no matter how dark life may seem, by asking God to help us see through His eyes. You know, when you're in the middle of a bad situation, you often can't see things the way they really are because your vision is blocked by hurt, fear, anger, and unforgiveness. The darkness can seem overwhelming, can't it? But with God's help, you can once again see things clearly. Ask Him to help you see your situation—no matter how dark it may be—through His eyes.

**DIGGING DEEPER:**

*Think back to a dark time in your life. Maybe a time when you felt angry or overlooked. How did you handle that darkness?*

**JURASSIC JOURNALING:**

*Sometimes it helps to write your feelings. Write God a letter, telling Him about the things in your life that seem pretty dark. Then ask for His help.*

# SAUROPELTA
## [SORE-oh-PEL-tah]

**BIBLE EXCAVATION:**

"I will answer them before they even call to me. While they are still talking about their needs, I will go ahead and answer their prayers!"

—ISAIAH 65:24 NLT

## STOP, DROP, AND PRAY!

The Sauropelta was an armored dinosaur with bony studs all over its back. It also had sharp spikes along each side of its body, beginning behind its eyes and continuing to its tail. You might say this guy was blinged out! But all that armor made this dino heavy and slow-moving. It couldn't outrun its enemies, so it had to come up with another plan for staying alive. Experts believe the Sauropelta probably crouched down low to protect the one place it wasn't heavily armored—its belly! Once the belly was protected, the Sauropelta would swing its head back and forth to stab at attackers. Pretty genius plan, right?

We can learn a lot from the Sauropelta. When trouble comes, our best line of defense is to drop to our knees and pray. Isaiah 65:24 says God hears our prayers before we even pray them. Of course, you don't have to *actually* be on your knees for God to hear your prayers. You can

### DINO STATS

**FAMILY:**
Nodosauridae

**HEIGHT:**
8 ft. (2.4 m)

**LENGTH:**
25 ft. (7.6 m)

**WEIGHT:**
4,000–6,000 lb. (1,814.4–2,721.6 kg)

**DIET:**
plants

DID YOU KNOW . . . that the name *Sauropelta* means "lizard shield"?

DIGGING DEEPER:

*Do you ever have trouble knowing what to pray? Just talk to God like you'd talk to your best friend. He can't wait to hear from you!*

## JURASSIC JOURNALING:

*Write about a time when you were facing something difficult and prayed to God about it and then He answered you in a big way. Try keeping a "prayer and praise" journal of when God answers your prayers, and then at the end of the year, read about what God has done for you!*

pray anytime, anywhere, and in any position. And you can trust that God hears and will answer.

If you don't know how to pray, it's always wise to pray things that agree with the Bible. If you're afraid, you could pray, "God, I feel scared, and I'm asking You to protect me as You promise in Your Word—to take away my fear and put Your love and courage there instead. I love You. Amen."

Remember, in the face of danger, "Stop, drop, and pray!"

# HYPSILOPHODON
## [hip-sill-OFF-oh-don]

**BIBLE EXCAVATION:**

[Love] always protects.

—1 CORINTHIANS 13:7 NIV

## DINO STATS

**FAMILY:**
Hypsilophodontidae

**HEIGHT:**
2 ft. (0.6 m)

**LENGTH:**
6 ft. (1.8 m)

**WEIGHT:**
150 lb. (68 kg)

**DIET:**
plants, possibly insects
and small reptiles

**DID YOU KNOW** . . . that the Hypsilophodon was one of the only dinosaurs to have cheeks? (Experts think it probably stored food in its cheeks while it chewed, much like humans do!)

# LOVE ALWAYS PROTECTS

The Hypsilophodon was a smaller dinosaur and hard to catch, especially because this dino wasn't alone. In fact, scientists believe they traveled in herds—mostly for protection against their enemies, the hungry Theropods. They looked out for one another and warned each other of danger. That helped these small dinos survive in a land of much bigger predators.

We can learn from these dinosaurs and their protective nature. As Christians, we should look out for our friends and family in this same way. We should be quick to warn them of danger when we see it. But that's not always how we behave, is it? Sometimes we operate by the world's standard that says, "If you don't look out for number one, who will?" But that's not God's way.

The Bible says we should put others' needs above our own (Philippians 2:4). It also says that we should walk in love and that love "always protects." So how can you do better at this? You can start with something small, like allowing your friends to go ahead of you in the lunch line at school. That would be a great way to put others' needs before your own. And the next time someone says something ugly about your best friend, stand up for her, but don't run and tell her about every ugly remark you hear. She doesn't need to know. Protect her from mean comments. And ask God to help you walk in love every day.

*Can you think of ways you can walk in love? Remember, love always protects.*

**JURASSIC JOURNALING:**

*In your Bible, find 1 Corinthians 13, also known as "the Love Chapter," and write out the first eight verses. Then try to memorize them!*

# MAIASAURA
## [MY-yah-SORE-ah]

## A GOOD FATHER

**DINO STATS**

**FAMILY:**
Hadrosauridae

**HEIGHT:**
8 ft. (2.4 m)

**LENGTH:**
30 ft. (9.1 m)

**WEIGHT:**
6,000–8,000 lb. (2,721.6– 3,628.7 kg)

**DIET:**
plants

**W**hen paleontologist Jack Horner explored a dinosaur nesting site in the Rocky Mountains of Montana, he learned a lot about the eggs and the dinosaurs who cared for those eggs. Each nest held about twenty eggs, but Horner also found fossils of baby dinosaurs up to about two months old in and around the nests. He then found evidence of food in the nests. This caused him to believe that the parent dinos had brought food to their babies. That's why Horner named these caring dinosaurs *Maiasaura*, meaning "good mother lizard."

The Maiasaura moms cared for their babies until they were sure those little dinos could take care of themselves. Some experts think the daddy dinosaurs also took care of the babies. This was unusual for dinosaurs—they weren't normally one big, happy family!

Aren't you glad it isn't unusual for God to take care of us? He is our heavenly Father, and He is really good at caring for His children! He loves us with an everlasting love, and He will take care of us our entire lives. The Bible

DIGGING DEEPER:

*What do you think are the most important qualities that a good father should have? Have you thanked your heavenly Father for being a good Dad?*

## JURASSIC JOURNALING:

*How has God, as your heavenly Father, provided for you recently? Write about the experience.*

says, "This same God who takes care of me will supply all your needs from his glorious riches, which have been given to us in Christ Jesus" (Philippians 4:19 NLT). He promises that He will never leave us or turn His back on us. He is a good Father, and you can trust Him.

 **DID YOU KNOW** . . . that a female fossil hunter, Laurie Trexler, discovered the Maiasaura?

# COMPSOGNATHUS
## [comp-sog-NAYTH-us]

BIBLE EXCAVATION:

We became like grasshoppers in our own sight, and so we were in their sight.

—NUMBERS 13:33 NASB

## GRASSHOPPER OR GIANT?

### DINO STATS

**FAMILY:**
Compsognathidae

**HEIGHT:**
10 in. (0.3 m)
at the hips

**LENGTH:**
3 ft. (0.9 m)

**WEIGHT:**
6.5 lb. (2.9 kg)

**DIET:**
mostly insects,
spiders, worms,
small lizards

The Compsognathus was tiny, no bigger than a large chicken or a small turkey. Small as it was, this dinosaur was just as fierce of a hunter as the much larger meat-eating dinosaurs. You know why?

Some research suggests that many of these dinos didn't know they were little because they were often the biggest dinosaurs in the area. They hunted small lizards, insects, spiders, and worms, so they towered over their food source. In other words, the Compsognathus was kind of a giant in its environment; therefore, it behaved as one.

It's all about how we see ourselves, isn't it? There's a story in the Bible that talks about this very thing. Moses sent twelve spies into the Promised Land to see if the land was good. When the spies came back, they all talked about how great the land was. But some also said that the people living there were stronger and bigger. "We were like grasshoppers compared to them," they reported. "We can't go there!" But two men, Joshua and Caleb, reported, "It's a great land! We can take it! Let's go!"

**DIGGING DEEPER:**

*What does it look like for someone to have "the God perspective" throughout the day?*

**JURASSIC JOURNALING:**

*You may not feel strong and powerful today, so what are some things you can do to build those feelings of strength and power in God? For example, maybe you could find Bible verses like "I can do all things through Christ who strengthens me" (Philippians 4:13 NKJV) and write them down.*

Joshua and Caleb didn't see themselves as small grasshoppers. They saw themselves as strong and powerful because they knew God was with them. We call that having "the God perspective." You have to see yourself as someone who can do all things with God, just like the Bible says. Take a lesson from Joshua, Caleb, and the Compsognathus. With God, you are strong and mighty, and you've got this!

**DID YOU KNOW** . . . that *Compsognathus* means "pretty jaw"?

# BARYONYX
[bah-ree-ON-ix]

"Come, follow me," Jesus said, "and I will send you out to fish for people."
—MATTHEW 4:19 NIV

## GONE FISHING

**DINO STATS**

**FAMILY:**
Spinosauridae

**HEIGHT:**
8–10 ft. (2.4–3 m)

**LENGTH:**
25–34 ft.
(7.6–10.4 m)

**WEIGHT:**
3,000–7,200
lb. (1,360.8–
3,265.9 kg)

**DIET:**
meat

With its long, skinny snout, the Baryonyx looked like a crocodile, and paleontologists think it was one of the largest fish-eating dinosaurs. Hanging out on a riverbank, this dinosaur probably reached its long neck out over the water and chomped down on fish that were swimming by. Or as some experts believe, it may have hunted like a bear, sweeping the river with its hook-like claws. Those claws were about 12 inches long! They worked perfectly as hooks, able to stab fish and scoop them into its mouth. You might say this dinosaur was quite the skilled fisherman.

You know, Jesus hung out with a lot of fishermen. In fact, four of the twelve disciples were fishermen—Peter, Andrew, James, and John. Maybe that's why Jesus chose to use these words when He called Peter and Andrew to be His disciples: "Follow me, and I will make you fishers of men" (Matthew 4:19 ESV). God has called us to be fishers of men too. But what exactly does that mean?

Bible experts believe Jesus is calling us to "catch" people for Him. In other words, we should share our

DIGGING DEEPER:

Have you ever told
somebody about Jesus?
Have you ever invited
anyone to church? If
you haven't, why not?

JURASSIC
JOURNALING:

Write the names of
five people you think
would like to be invited
to church or hear more
about Jesus in the near
future.

faith in Jesus with others. We don't need a
12-inch claw or a long, crocodile-like snout to
do that—thank goodness! We just need the
courage to tell others about Jesus. So go ahead.
Be a fisher of men!

DID YOU KNOW . . . that partially digested remains of ancient
fish and remains of a young Iguanodon were found inside
the stomach of a Baryonyx specimen from England?

# XIAOTINGIA
## [shyOW-TIN-gee-uh]

[God] anointed us, set his seal of ownership on us, and put his Spirit in our hearts as a deposit, guaranteeing what is to come.

—2 CORINTHIANS 1:21–22 NIV

## DINO STATS

**FAMILY:**
Dromaeosauridae

**HEIGHT:**
1 ft. (0.3 m)

**LENGTH:**
2 ft. (0.6 m)

**WEIGHT:**
5 lb. (2.3 kg)

**DIET:**
mostly insects

**DID YOU KNOW** . . . that the Xiaotingia ate not only insects but occasionally some shellfish and plants too?

# WHO ARE YOU?

The Xiaotingia has been the topic of many fights between paleontologists over the years. Some are sure this creature was a bird and not a dinosaur at all. But others are positive the Xiaotingia was definitely a dinosaur with bird-like features. This creature, whether it was a bird or a bird-like dinosaur, wasn't very big. It was only about the size of a chicken with a really long tail. Experts believe it could fly short distances but mostly walked to get places. Even today, the very mention of this dinosaur sparks a debate. Is it a bird? Is it a dinosaur? It just depends on who you ask.

The Xiaotingia's place in history hasn't been decided yet. Various scientists continue fighting over the right to define this bird/dino creature. And it may never be settled.

Aren't you glad that your identity isn't up for debate? You are a child of God, and you have a very special identity. You have the imprint of our heavenly Father in your DNA. Pretty cool, huh? Your place in history has already been decided—by Almighty God—and that's not up for debate.

## DIGGING DEEPER:

*Have you thought about how you have your heavenly Father's DNA inside of you? Knowing that amazing fact, how does that make you feel about yourself and your future?*

## JURASSIC JOURNALING:

*Pretend you're a reporter covering important people in history, and you've been assigned to write about you. Now write an article about the future you—all of the things you accomplished in your life.*

# PEGOMASTAX
## [PEG-oh-MAST-ax]

The peace of God, which surpasses all understanding,
will guard your hearts and your minds in Christ Jesus.

—PHILIPPIANS 4:7 ESV

## DINO STATS

**FAMILY:**
Heterodontosauridae

**HEIGHT:**
2 ft. (0.6 m)

**LENGTH:**
23 in. (0.6 m)

**WEIGHT:**
5 lb. (2.3 kg)

**DIET:**
plants

## PUT AWAY THOSE BRISTLES

The Pegomastax had vampire-like fangs, a parrot-looking beak, and tough quills covering its body. Let's just say if there had been a dinosaur beauty pageant, the Pegomastax probably wouldn't have won. Scientists have wondered why the Pegomastax, a plant-eater, had such long, sharp fangs, but some believe this little guy also munched on insects and rotting flesh from other animals. Plus, Pego might've used the fangs when protecting itself against an enemy or when fighting for a mate.

While a full-grown Pegomastax weighed less than a cat, its porcupine-like bristles made this little dinosaur look pretty intimidating and likely kept predators away.

We humans have been known to wear bristles from time to time—maybe not on the outside, but on the inside, covering our hearts. It's the way we protect our hearts from hurt or pain.

DID YOU KNOW . . . that *Pegomastax* means "thick or strong jaw"?

## DIGGING DEEPER:

*How have you been hurt by someone recently? Has that caused you not to trust others?*

## JURASSIC JOURNALING:

*It's been said that hurting people often hurt people. Maybe the person who hurt your feelings is someone who is also hurting. Write a prayer in your journal for this person.*

Have you ever worn bristles around your heart? You might put them there when you've been hurt by a friend or loved one. Rather than let yourself get hurt again, you put up those protective quills. You might not even be aware that you're "bristling," yet those imaginary bristles keep everybody out of your life and heart. It happens to all of us, but it's time to break free of those quills and let God into your heart. He can heal past hurts, and you can trust Him. He won't ever hurt you, let you down, or leave you. He adores you, and that love is a forever kind of love that will help the bristles fall off and never grow back.

# NIGERSAURUS
## [NEE-jer-SORE-us]

BIBLE EXCAVATION:

Do not be afraid or discouraged, for the LORD will personally go ahead of you. He will be with you; he will neither fail you nor abandon you.
—DEUTERONOMY 31:8 NLT

## DINO STATS

**FAMILY:**
Rebbachisauridae

**HEIGHT:**
8 ft. (2.4 m)
at the hips

**LENGTH:**
30 ft. (9.1 m)

**WEIGHT:**
3,800–10,000 lb.
(1,723.7–4,535.9 kg)

**DIET:**
plants

# FOLLOW YOUR PATH

The Nigersaurus was a strange-looking dinosaur! Scientists believe it had a flat, nozzle-shaped mouth and a rather short neck, which made reaching leaves on the taller trees impossible. Instead, this dino dropped its head and swayed its neck back and forth, acting like a living vacuum cleaner.

Paleontologist Paul Sereno discovered the fossils of the Nigersaurus in northwestern Africa. The locals call this area *Gadoufaoua*, which means "the place where camels fear to tread." I don't know about you, but going to a place called "the place where camels fear to tread" would not be my first choice. I mean, that's probably not a future vacation spot, know what I'm saying?

It's funny. Sometimes God will lead you to places you wouldn't have chosen to go, but because He is leading the way, amazing discoveries will be there. I'm guessing if Paul Sereno could've discovered dinosaur fossils on a beach in Florida, he might've gone there instead of "the place where camels fear to tread." But he made an uncomfortable trip through Gadoufaoua, and it was well worth it because of the important dino discoveries awaiting him there.

So don't be afraid to go places that might seem scary at first. If you're following the path God has for your life, you don't have to worry. The Bible says that God goes before you, so that means He's already been there! You have the perfect travel guide as you go through life. So follow God and get ready for some amazing discoveries!

### DIGGING DEEPER:

*Think of a time when you were nervous about going somewhere new, but once you got there, you were glad you went. We've all experienced that before! The key is to trust God in every decision. If you feel He is leading you, then go!*

### JURASSIC JOURNALING:

*Write about a place you'd love to go or something you'd love to do—even if some people think it would be scary.*

DID YOU KNOW . . . that the mouth of the Nigersaurus was the widest part of its head?

# LATIRHINUS
## [la-ti-RIEN-us]

We are confident of all this because of our great trust in God through Christ. It is not that we think we are qualified to do anything on our own. Our qualification comes from God.

—2 CORINTHIANS 3:4–5 NLT

# BIG NOSE, DON'T CARE

## DINO STATS

**FAMILY:**
Hadrosauridae

**HEIGHT:**
5–6 ft. (1.5–1.8 m)

**LENGTH:**
29.5 ft. (9 m)

**WEIGHT:**
6,000 lb.
(2,721.6 kg)

**DIET:**
plants

When the Latirhinus was first discovered, the headlines read, "New Dinosaur Discovered in Mexico Had a Gigantic Nose." How would you like to be known for that? Apparently its extra-large nose made up almost half of this dinosaur's head. Experts also believe this huge nose had a flap of loose skin that could blow up like a balloon and make a honking noise. While we might think a large nose with a honking flap of skin sounds really gross, the Latirhinus used it to his advantage. In fact, this dinosaur used its nose to show off to find a dino date.

Strange as it might sound, the trait you dislike about yourself or the thing that you feel is holding you back from being good at something might just be what God will use to your advantage! For example, actor Bruce Willis had a severe stutter when he was in school. You wouldn't think that someone who stuttered would be able to be a movie star, but that's just what happened! Because he stuttered, he learned to make people laugh, and that ability helped

## DIGGING DEEPER:

*Can you think of more people who have had obstacles and turned those negatives into positives? What kind of attitude does someone need to turn a disadvantage into an advantage?*

## JURASSIC JOURNALING:

*Write a prayer to God, thanking Him for all the qualities that make you unique.*

him do well in Hollywood. Or consider Fanny Crosby, a little girl who became blind when she was six weeks old. Because she couldn't see, she learned to use her imagination and describe things with great detail. She used this ability to write more than nine thousand songs!

So what is holding you back? Take a look at what you think is a disadvantage and ask God to use it in a positive way in your life.

 DID YOU KNOW . . . that *Latirhinus* means "wide or broad nose"?

# ALECTROSAURUS
## [ah-LEC-tro-SORE-us]

**BIBLE EXCAVATION:**

LORD, you have examined me and know all about me. You know when I sit down and when I get up. You know my thoughts before I think them. You know where I go and where I lie down. You know everything I do.

—PSALM 139:1–3 NCV

## DINO STATS

**FAMILY:**
Tyrannosauridae

**HEIGHT:**
6–8 ft. (1.8–2.4 m)

**LENGTH:**
30 ft. (9.1 m)

**WEIGHT:**
1,000–3,200 lb.
(453.6–1,451.5 kg)

**DIET:**
meat

# HE KNOWS YOU!

The Alectrosaurus is sort of a mystery dinosaur. Scientists know very little about this dino because very few fossils have been recovered. In 1923, George Olsen discovered the first Alectrosaurus fossil, but this dinosaur wasn't named until 1933. And the only things we know for sure are that this dinosaur looked a little like a Tyrannosaurus Rex (only smaller), it lived in Asia, and it was a fast, skilled hunter, preying on Oviraptors.

Aren't you glad you're better known than the Alectrosaurus? Isn't it nice that your family knows all about you—your likes and dislikes, your favorite food, your biggest fear, the name of your best friend? But there's someone else who knows you even better—your heavenly Father. That's right, God knows every detail about you. After all, He made you! He not only knows who you are. He knows where you are, your hopes and dreams, and exactly what you're going through at this very moment. He even knows all your flaws, and He loves you just the same.

**DIGGING DEEPER:**

*Do people really know you, or are you pretty mysterious like the Alectrosaurus? If you answered "mysterious," why do you think you're hard to get to know?*

**JURASSIC JOURNALING:**

*Write five facts that people don't know about you that you wish they knew. Now look through all of the "Bible Excavation" sections of this book and find three facts about God that you didn't know before.*

You can get to know God too. The way to do that is by reading the Bible and praying to Him every day. He wants you to know Him just like you know your best friend. So spend some time with Him today, and get to know Him. It's the most important relationship you'll ever have.

**DID YOU KNOW . . .** that *Alectrosaurus* means "lonely lizard"?

# RHAMPHORHYNCHUS
## [RAM-foe-RINK-us]

**BIBLE EXCAVATION:**

Be alert and of sober mind. Your enemy the devil prowls
around like a roaring lion looking for someone to devour.

—1 PETER 5:8 NIV

## BE ON GUARD!

**DINO STATS**

**FAMILY:**
Rhamphorhynchidae

**HEIGHT:**
11–14 in. (0.3–0.4 m)

**LENGTH:**
20 in. (0.5 m)

**WEIGHT:**
1–2 lb. (0.5–0.9 kg)

**DIET:**
mostly fish, some
insects and frogs

The Rhamphorhynchus is often pictured as a large, ferocious, bird-like, flying reptile with scary, sharp teeth, but actually it was the size of a pigeon. Not too intimidating. However, it did have a **wingspan** of three feet. That's pretty impressive for such a small body!

Scientists believe the Rhamphorhynchus would swoop down over the water, scoop up fish, and chow down. But once in a while, the Rhamphorhynchus got too close to the water while searching for food and became a meal for a large, hungry fish. They were so focused on finding food that they forgot to protect themselves from *becoming* food. You might say they let their guard down.

That didn't end well for the Rhamphorhynchus, and it won't turn out well for us either. The Bible tells us to be alert because the Devil, our enemy, prowls around like a lion in search of someone to devour! Now, we don't have to be afraid of this because God is on our side and He

DIGGING DEEPER:

Do you ever thank God for His protection? You should! Thank Him now for always watching over you.

JURASSIC JOURNALING:

Write about a time when God kept you from harm.

DINO DICTIONARY:

**wingspan**—the distance between the ends of an animal's wings.

has already defeated the Devil. But that won't stop the Devil from trying to trap us and make our lives difficult until we get to heaven. So be alert! That means "be watchful." For example, if someone dares you to steal a pack of gum, your "on guard" sensors should go off. It might seem like a harmless prank, but that "harmless prank" goes against God's Word—and it's against the law!

Be prayed up. Pray Psalm 91 over your life every day and thank God for His protection and direction. Don't be afraid; just be alert. There's a difference.

DID YOU KNOW . . . that the Rhamphorhynchus had a very long tail that acted like a ship's rudder?

# DEINONYCHUS
## [dye-NON-ik-us]

**BIBLE EXCAVATION:**

Don't copy the behavior and customs of this world, but let God transform you into a new person by changing the way you think. Then you will learn to know God's will for you, which is good and pleasing and perfect.

—ROMANS 12:2 NLT

## DINO STATS

**FAMILY:**
Dromaeosauridae

**HEIGHT:**
5 ft. (1.5 m)

**LENGTH:**
3–10 ft. (0.9–3 m)

**WEIGHT:**
110–175 lb.
(49.9–79.4 kg)

**DIET:**
meat

# ARE YOU IN CAMO?

John Ostrom's study of the Deinonychus in 1964 was a very big deal. Up until that time, paleontologists thought meat-eating dinos were all slow, stupid, and clumsy. But after Ostrom named the dino *Deinonychus,* meaning "terrible claw," and described it as fierce, other scientists learned that meat-eating dinos could be fast, smart, and cunning.

Experts think the Deinonychus was a master of disguise, blending into its surroundings and hiding. No one knows for sure whether the Deinonychus had scaly skin or feathers, but either way, their covering helped conceal them. They could hide from their predators, and they could also stay hidden until it was the perfect time to surprise their prey.

Do you ever try to hide in your surroundings? Do you ever try to blend in with the crowd because it's safer? There are times when we all do that for different reasons, sometimes to avoid being made fun of. We laugh at a mean joke because if we don't blend in, we'll feel awkward and out of place. But God wants us to stand up for what we believe and do the right thing. Sometimes standing up means standing out, and that's okay.

## DIGGING DEEPER:

*Think of a time when you tried to blend in with the crowd. Now ask God to help you step out in faith to do the right thing, no matter what everyone else is doing.*

## JURASSIC JOURNALING:

*Create a fun saying or short rhyme about standing out, and write it in your journal.*

 DID YOU KNOW . . . that the Deinonychus had retractable claws like a cat?

# MUSSAURUS
## [moose-SORE-us]

**BIBLE EXCAVATION:**

He put another parable before them, saying, "The kingdom of heaven is like a grain of mustard seed that a man took and sowed in his field. It is the smallest of all seeds, but when it has grown it is larger than all the garden plants and becomes a tree, so that the birds of the air come and make nests in its branches."

—MATTHEW 13:31–32 ESV

## SMALL BEGINNINGS, BIG RESULTS

### DINO STATS

**FAMILY:**
Mussauridae

**HEIGHT:**
10 ft. (3 m)

**LENGTH:**
10 ft. (3 m)

**WEIGHT:**
150–260 lb.
(68–117.9 kg)

**DIET:**
plants

Can you imagine a 260-pound dinosaur coming from an egg no bigger than a common sparrow's egg? The big Mussaurus had such small beginnings. When its hatchling remains were first discovered in 1979, it was called the "world's smallest dinosaur"—but that wasn't exactly true. Later research proved that the average Mussaurus adult probably weighed over 150 pounds and was 10 feet long. The tiniest dino was the Anchiornis Huxleyi, which was only 16 inches long.

Still, the fact that such a large dinosaur could come from such a tiny egg is interesting. If we had been around to watch this dino grow up, we'd probably be pretty amazed at how big God created this dinosaur to be! God can take something small and make something quite big and impressive out of it. He even talks about

**DID YOU KNOW** . . . that *Mussaurus* means "mouse lizard"?

that in the Bible. Matthew 17:20 says, "If you have faith as small as a mustard seed, you can say to this mountain, 'Move from here to there,' and it will move. Nothing will be impossible for you" (NIV). In other words, out of something so small—faith as small as a mustard seed—God can produce big miracles.

So if you feel too little or too young to do big things for God, don't worry. God can use you right now! You could send thank-you cards to military men and women serving our country. Or you could organize a group of kids and do yard work for some of the disabled or elderly people in your neighborhood. You're not too little to do big things with God.

# DIPLODOCUS
## [dih-PLOD-uh-kus]

BIBLE EXCAVATION:

Carry each other's burdens, and in this way you will fulfill the law of Christ.

—GALATIANS 6:2 NIV

# NEED A LIFT?

## DINO STATS

**FAMILY:**
Diplodocidae

**HEIGHT:**
16 ft. (4.9 m)

**LENGTH:**
80–175 ft.
(24.4–53.3 m)

**WEIGHT:**
24,000–30,000
lb. (10,886.2–
13,607.8 kg)

**DIET:**
plants

The Diplodocus is one of the longest dinosaurs to have ever roamed the earth. It had a unique body, with a very long neck and a very long tail. Under that tail were two rows of bones to support all the weight—those tail bones weighed about 3,500 pounds by themselves! This extremely long dino got its name *Diplodocus*—which means "double beam"—because of the double row of bones in its tail, like a double beam. Some have compared this dinosaur's build to a giant suspension bridge set between four ginormous pillars. It needed this bridge-like build in order to support its heavy body.

You know, everyone needs extra support once in a while. When life's problems get too heavy to handle alone, you can turn to God. The Bible says to cast your cares on Him (1 Peter 5:7). That means when you're worrying about that big math test or you're concerned about your grandmother's illness, you can put all those cares right over onto God. So pray about all your troubles—He can take it, and what's more, He wants to replace your worries with peace!

We should also lift each other up when life gets "heavy." If you know your best friend is stressed out because his parents have been fighting a lot, you can lift him up in prayer. You can be there when he needs

**DIGGING DEEPER:**

*What are some ways you can support people in your life who may be carrying around a heavy load of worries right now?*

**JURASSIC JOURNALING:**

*Draw a picture of a long bridge and then write, "Cast all of your cares on God" over the top of it as a reminder that God has got you.*

to talk and let him know he isn't carrying that heavy load all by himself. Let God be that extra support in your life, and then offer that same support to others.

**DID YOU KNOW** . . . that fossils of the Diplodocus were found in Colorado, Utah, and Wyoming?

# LYCAENOPS
## [LY-can-ops]

BIBLE EXCAVATION:

It's better to have a partner than go it alone. Share the work, share the wealth. And if one falls down, the other helps, but if there's no one to help, tough! ... By yourself you're unprotected. With a friend you can face the worst. Can you round up a third? A three-stranded rope isn't easily snapped.

—ECCLESIASTES 4:9–10, 12 MSG

# FIND YOUR PACK

## DINO STATS

**FAMILY:**
Gorgonopsidae

**HEIGHT:**
3 ft. (0.9 m)

**LENGTH:**
3–4 ft. (0.9–1.2 m)

**WEIGHT:**
20–30 lb.
(9.1–13.6 kg)

**DIET:**
meat

The Lycaenops is thought to be a reptile-like mammal with two long, fang-like canine teeth. Paleontologists believe it was not much bigger than a fox, but it was mean and aggressive like a wolverine. They also think this dino was much like a wolf, not only in its appearance but also in the way it hunted. The Lycaenops hunted in packs and could take down much larger animals by working together. They traveled in packs for protection against bigger predators. Alone, the Lycaenops was an easy target, but with its pack, a predator was less likely to attack and have to fight an entire group of angry dinos.

They needed each other to survive and thrive, and guess what? So do we.

Have you ever heard the saying "Find your tribe. Love them hard"? God wants you to love your tribe, help your tribe, and grow with your tribe. We need to take care of our tribe and allow them to care for us. We need to encourage them when they feel down, and we need to offer advice when we see them going in the wrong direction.

But who's in your tribe? That's the fun part—you get to choose your own tribe. So find a pack of Christians and become a tribe. Start a prayer group that meets before school. Find other Christians in your neighborhood, clubs, sports teams, or school, and start building that tribe. Together, you'll be strong. Together, you'll grow. Together, you'll be able to accomplish a lot for God.

**DID YOU KNOW** . . . that the name *Lycaenops* means "wolf face"?

# TYRANNOSAURUS REX
## [tie-RAN-oh-SORE-us REX]

BIBLE EXCAVATION:

All Scripture is inspired by God and is useful to teach us what is true and to make us realize what is wrong in our lives. It corrects us when we are wrong and teaches us to do what is right. God uses it to prepare and equip his people to do every good work.

—2 TIMOTHY 3:16–17 NLT

## DINO STATS

**FAMILY:**
Tyrannosauridae

**HEIGHT:**
13 ft. (4 m)

**LENGTH:**
40 ft. (12.2 m)

**WEIGHT:**
14,000 lb.
(6,350.3 kg)

**DIET:**
other dinosaurs
(bones and all!)

# EAT EVERY DAY

Scientists believe the T. Rex was one of the scariest dinosaurs to walk the planet. It had a very deadly bite. Experts say it could eat more than 500 pounds of meat in just one chomp! An enormous beast, the T. Rex feasted on large plant-eating dinosaurs.

But it didn't eat every day. It didn't have to. In fact, scientists say that after eating a large plant-eating dinosaur, the T. Rex could go several weeks without having to eat again. Can you imagine only having to eat once every few weeks?

Although humans can technically go without food for thirty to forty days and still survive—as long as we drink plenty of water—it's not advised. We need to eat daily to keep our physical bodies energetic and healthy. We need to eat so that all our systems can do what they are supposed to do.

But fruits and vegetables aren't the only food we need. We also need to "eat" God's Word every day to be

**DIGGING DEEPER:**

*How often do you read your Bible? Have you set aside a certain time each day to spend with God? If you haven't yet, are you willing to do so?*

**JURASSIC JOURNALING:**

*Using your journal, plan a menu for the next week—physical and spiritual food. So maybe on Monday you eat pepperoni pizza and read John 3:16. Happy "meal" planning!*

spiritually healthy. That's why Matthew 6:11 says, "Give us this day our daily bread" (NKJV) instead of "Give us this day our monthly bread." We need a helping of God's Word every single day if we want to grow strong in faith. So eat up! Read God's Word today and every day.

**DID YOU KNOW** . . . that the T. Rex had sixty razor-sharp, banana-size teeth?

# PSITTACOSAURUS
## [SIT-uh-kO-SORE-us]

For You, O Lᴏʀᴅ, will bless the righteous; with favor You will surround him as with a shield.

—PSALM 5:12 ɴᴋᴊᴠ

## YOU'RE THE FAVORITE

### DINO STATS

**FAMILY:**
Psittacosauridae

**HEIGHT:**
4 ft. (1.2 m)

**LENGTH:**
6–7 ft. (1.8–2.1 m)

**WEIGHT:**
50–175 lb.
(22.7 79.4 kg)

**DIET:**
plants

The Psittacosaurus had a head that looked like a cross between a turtle and a parrot. It was a strange-looking creature with horns on its cheeks, and it had long toes and sharp claws, probably used for digging. Its front legs were shorter than its back legs, and scientists believe this dino could have run about 40 miles per hour!

Henry Fairfield Osborn named the Psittacosaurus in 1923. He also named the Tyrannosaurus Rex eighteen years earlier, along with several other dinosaurs. Obviously the T. Rex is a much more famous dino than the Psittacosaurus, and I'm guessing the T. Rex was Osborn's favorite. The T. Rex was bigger, more ferocious, scarier, and far more interesting than the parrot-looking dinosaur.

Have you ever felt like you're *not* the favorite in your family? Well, I have good news for you. Even if you had a sibling as famous as the T. Rex, you'd still be God's favorite. He adores you!

God shows His ultimate favor through the gift of His Son, Jesus, who died on the cross for our sins so

**DIGGING DEEPER:**

*Do you ever get jealous of others because of the good things God has given them? You shouldn't, because God has enough favor to go around. Say a prayer, thanking God that He blesses you and others.*

**JURASSIC JOURNALING:**

*Write about a time when you experienced something really great, even though you knew you didn't deserve it. Explain how you knew it was "a God thing."*

that we could spend eternity in heaven. But He also shows us favor through unexpected gifts, encouragement, protection, and so much more. And because you're highly favored, you should thank God for His special gifts. Whenever you experience unexpected good things, just look up and say, "Thanks, God. I know that was You." It's important to praise Him for His favor, so make it a habit to thank God every time you realize that God adores you.

DID YOU KNOW . . . that a baby Psittacosaurus was barely longer than a human hand when it hatched?

# BRONTOSAURUS
## [BRONT-oh-SORE-us]

**BIBLE EXCAVATION:**

You watched me as I was being formed in utter seclusion, as I was woven together in the dark of the womb. You saw me before I was born. Every day of my life was recorded in your book. Every moment was laid out before a single day had passed.

—PSALM 139:15–16 NLT

## DINO STATS

**FAMILY:**
Diplodocidae

**HEIGHT:**
15–18 ft.
(4.6–5.5 m)

**LENGTH:**
70–90 ft.
(21.3–27.4 m)

**WEIGHT:**
34,000–76,000 lb. (15,422.1–34,473 kg)

**DIET:**
plants

**DID YOU KNOW** . . . that the name *Brontosaurus* means "thunder lizard"?

# YOU ARE NOT A MISTAKE

In 1877, Othniel Marsh discovered the Brontosaurus. At the time, he was competing with another paleontologist, Edward Cope, to find the most dinosaurs. In his rush to discover more dinosaurs than Cope, Marsh failed to realize the Brontosaurus was the same species he had discovered two years earlier and named the "Apatosaurus." It wasn't until 1903 that this mistake was discovered, causing the first name—the Apatosaurus—to become the official name of this giant Sauropod dinosaur.

But the Brontosaurus may have the last laugh. In 2015, a group of scientists found evidence that the Brontosaurus and the Apatosaurus are different after all. In addition, scientists now think there might be three species of Brontosaurus: *Brontosaurus excelsus*, *Brontosaurus parvus*, and *Brontosaurus yahnahpin*.

Imagine if you were like the Brontosaurus. First, you're a big deal—everyone is talking about you. Then, you're ignored, and it feels as if you never existed, and some say you're just a big mistake. Later, people act like you're important once again. What a crazy ride for our friend the Brontosaurus!

The Bronto wasn't a mistake—and you aren't either! There's never been any confusion about who you are or who you're called to be. You see, God has had a plan for your life since before you were born. Isn't that exciting? If you'll trust God and stay close to Him, He will guide you all the days of your life. The Creator of the universe has big plans for you—even bigger than the Brontosaurus!

**DIGGING DEEPER:**

*Have you ever wondered why you're here on earth? What do you think you'll be doing twenty years from now? Ask God to show you.*

**JURASSIC JOURNALING:**

*Write three ways you can grow closer to God.*

# DILOPHOSAURUS
## [di-LOWF-oh-SORE-us]

**BIBLE EXCAVATION:**

You are tempted in the same way that everyone else is tempted.
But God can be trusted not to let you be tempted too much,
and he will show you how to escape from your temptations.

—1 CORINTHIANS 10:13 CEV

## DINO STATS

**FAMILY:**
Dilophosauridae

**HEIGHT:**
10 ft. (3 m)

**LENGTH:**
23 ft. (7 m)

**WEIGHT:**
900 lb. (408.2 kg)

**DIET:**
meat

## RUN AWAY

**W**eighing about as much as a large polar bear, the Dilophosaurus was one of the biggest meat-eating dinosaurs to roam the earth. And that's not all—it had two bony crests on top of its head, making it appear even bigger and scarier than it was. Scientists think these crests might have been covered with brightly colored skin, which would have made them stand out even more.

Some scientists think the Dilophosaurus used those crests to intimidate its enemies. Apparently, this sly dino would display its crest, trying to make the enemy afraid so it would run. Pretty clever, right? In reality, those crests weren't a weapon of any sort. In fact, they were too thin to use for head-butting, and the crests didn't shoot poisonous venom (like some movies have shown). They were just there for show. Sometimes this little stunt worked, and sometimes it didn't. When it didn't work,

**DID YOU KNOW . . .** that in some dinosaur movies the Dilophosaurus is shown spitting poison, but there is no proof that this dino could spray venom?

the Dilophosaurus had a way of escape. Though it was large, it could run about 20 miles per hour. So it ran away.

Maybe that doesn't seem very brave, but sometimes running away is the smartest thing to do. Let's say you have been trying to stop talking about other people, but one of your friends sits by you at lunch and starts gossiping. You try to change the subject. You try to ignore her. But she just keeps on talking about all your other friends. In that situation, take a lesson from the Dilophosaurus and run away.

# HADROSAURUS
## [HAD-ruh-SORE-us]

BIBLE EXCAVATION:

"I am about to do something new. See, I have already begun! Do you not see it?"

—ISAIAH 43:19 NLT

## DINO STATS

**FAMILY:**
Hadrosauridae

**HEIGHT:**
15 ft. (4.6 m)

**LENGTH:**
23–33 ft.
(7–10.1 m)

**WEIGHT:**
6,000 lb.
(2,721.6 kg)

**DIET:**
plants

 DID YOU KNOW . . . that the name *Hadrosaurus* means "sturdy lizard"?

# MAKE ROOM FOR THE NEW!

The Hadrosaur group of dinosaurs is often called "the duckbills" because of their beak-like mouths. While this dino didn't have any teeth in the front of its beak, it had hundreds of tiny teeth packed into the back of its mouth. These teeth were perfect for grinding up tough plants and pinecones.

Not only did the Hadrosaurus have perfect teeth for chewing tough plants, but it also had the ability to replace those teeth when they were too ground down to be effective. Isn't that cool? They were continually growing new teeth to replace their old ones.

It works that way in humans too, but we only replace our teeth once. You lose your baby teeth to make room for your permanent teeth. The big, beautiful permanent teeth can't grow in until your baby teeth get out of the way. This same principle also applies in your spiritual life—the God part of you. God has big, beautiful, new things planned for your life, but if you are too scared to try new things, you'll only have your spiritual baby teeth. Maybe you're too nervous to pray out loud in front of people, yet you feel in your heart that God would like you to do that. Or maybe you know you're a great singer, but you're too nervous to sing a special song in church—still, you think you're supposed to. Trust God and ask Him to help you be brave enough to step out of your comfort zone. Get rid of those spiritual baby teeth, and make room for those beautiful new permanent teeth.

## DIGGING DEEPER:

*What are some new things you feel God calling you to do?*

## JURASSIC JOURNALING:

*Write some things that might be keeping you from trying new things or growing. Now write, "Make room for the new!" over the top of those things.*

# TRICERATOPS
[try-SERR-ah-tops]

We have this hope as an anchor for the soul, firm and secure.
—HEBREWS 6:19 NIV

## WHERE'S YOUR HOPE?

**DINO STATS**

**FAMILY:**
Ceratopsidae

**HEIGHT:**
9–10 ft. (2.7–3 m)

**LENGTH:**
30 ft. (9.1 m)

**WEIGHT:**
20,000 lb.
(9,071.8 kg)

**DIET:**
plants

The Triceratops is one of the best-known dinosaurs of all time. It's also one of the most studied dinos. Because of that, we know quite a bit about this horn-faced dinosaur. For instance, we know that its beak, head, and neck **frill** made up almost a quarter of its entire length! And we know it weighed about as much as a very large elephant. We also know its mouth was toothless, but it had lots of sharp teeth in its cheeks. It needed all those teeth for chewing tough plants. Scientists think the dino's neck frill may have acted as an anchor for the dinosaur's powerful jaw muscles that enabled it to chew such tough plant matter.

Did you know the Bible says that hope is our anchor? Hope does for our soul what an anchor does for a ship. It holds it in place. No matter how hard the wind blows or how many waves smack up against a ship, that anchor holds it secure. It's the same way in our Christian lives. No matter what difficult situations come our way—even the ones that seem so hard we feel shaken up—our hope in God holds us secure. That's why it's so important to place your hope in God alone. He will never let you down. You can trust Him.

## DIGGING DEEPER:

*Have you ever placed your hope in something or someone other than God? If so, how did that turn out for you?*

## JURASSIC JOURNALING:

*Write the letters H-O-P-E down the left side of your paper. Now write a word or phrase beginning with each letter that describes how hope makes you feel.*

## DINO DICTIONARY:

**frill**—*an extra fan-like feature on the back of some reptiles' heads.*

 DID YOU KNOW . . . that the Triceratops is thought to have lived alone, not in herds, like many other dinosaurs?

# SHANTUNGOSAURUS
[shan-TUNG-oh-SORE-us]

**BIBLE EXCAVATION:**

I can do all this through him who gives me strength.
—PHILIPPIANS 4:13 NIV

## DINO STATS

**FAMILY:**
Hadrosauridae

**HEIGHT:**
25 ft. (7.6 m)

**LENGTH:**
48–52 ft.
(14.6–15.8 m)

**WEIGHT:**
29,400 lb.
(13,335.6 kg)

**DIET:**
plants

## YOU CAN DO THE IMPOSSIBLE!

Possibly the largest of all the duck-billed dinosaurs—weighing more than two African bush elephants—the Shantungosaurus was rather gentle. It probably spent most of its time on all fours, but scientists believe this enormous dino was able to run on its back two legs when trying to escape a predator. Can you imagine the loud thuds each step must've made as this 14-ton dinosaur made its escape? It seems physically impossible that a creature so large could support itself on its back legs and actually run, doesn't it? Yet many paleontologists say it could do just that!

Is there something you want to do that seems impossible? The secret to achieving goals that seem impossible is simple, really. Create habits that will lead to success. For example, if you dream of making straight As this semester yet you're far from reaching that goal, start moving in that direction today. Study thirty more minutes each night. Make plans to join a study group at

**DIGGING DEEPER:**

*Think of your three top goals you wish to accomplish. What's preventing you from reaching those goals?*

**JURASSIC JOURNALING:**

*Have you ever heard the saying "Luck is where hard work meets opportunity"? It's true! So write two or three things you plan to do this week to move you toward your goals.*

school. Ask your teacher if there are any tutors who can help you with your most difficult classes. But most importantly, keep a positive attitude as you move toward that goal. Share your goal with others who will support you, and ask God to help you. If the Shantungosaurus can run on its back two legs, you can do what seems impossible too!

**DID YOU KNOW** . . . that the Shantungosaurus had a toothless beak and jaws that contained around fifteen hundred tiny teeth?

# THERIZINOSAURUS
## [THER-uh-ZEEN-oh-SORE-us]

If anyone is in Christ, the new creation has come: The old has gone, the new is here!

—2 CORINTHIANS 5:17 NIV

## A NEW CREATURE

### DINO STATS

**FAMILY:**
Therizinosauridae

**HEIGHT:**
10–15 ft. (3–4.6 m)

**LENGTH:**
23–33 ft.
(7–10.1 m)

**WEIGHT:**
1,000  6,000 lb.
(453.6–2,721.6 kg)

**DIET:**
plants, insects

When the Therizinosaurus was first discovered in 1954, the Russian paleontologist thought it was a sea turtle, not a dinosaur. It wasn't until the 1970s when a new group of fossils was found that this beast was recognized as a dinosaur. And it was a funny-looking creature for sure! Scientists think they stood on their back legs and had very wide hips, a pot belly, a short tail, feathers, and the longest claws of any known animal. It was a strange dinosaur, yes, but still a dinosaur.

Let's face it—a sea turtle and a dinosaur are very different creatures. They would've behaved differently, eaten different things, and probably lived in different areas. Had they been side by side, it would've been obvious they were different creatures. You know, before we accept Jesus into our hearts, we are very different too, almost as different as a sea turtle is from a dinosaur. The Bible talks about becoming a new creature in 2 Corinthians 5:17: "If anyone is in Christ, the new creation has come: The old has gone, the new is here!" (NIV).

What are some ways you've changed since becoming a new creature in Christ?

Write about the areas in your life that might still need changing. Then write a prayer asking God to help you improve in those areas. He will!

So here's a question for you—since you gave your life to God, do you behave differently? Are you kinder to your family members? Do you get angry less often? Are you more patient with your baby brother? If you haven't changed that much since you became a new creature in Christ, ask God to make those changes in your life.

DID YOU KNOW . . . that the claws of the Therizinosaurus were as long as short swords?

# MUTTABURRASAURUS
## [mutt-ah-BUHR-ah-SORE-us]

**BIBLE EXCAVATION:**

God thinks of us as a perfume that brings Christ to everyone.

—2 CORINTHIANS 2:15 CEV

## DINO STATS

**FAMILY:**
Iguanodontidae

**HEIGHT:**
8–15 ft.
(2.4–4.6 m)

**LENGTH:**
23–26 ft. (7–7.9 m)

**WEIGHT:**
6,200 lb.
(2,812.3 kg)

**DIET:**
plants, possibly
some meat

# SMELL YA LATER

This dinosaur, which had a bony beak and very sharp teeth, was believed to be a plant-eater. However, a few paleontologists think the Muttaburrasaurus might also have eaten dead animals from time to time. It was a very interesting dinosaur. In fact, this dino had a bony bump on its snout between its eyes and its mouth, and scientists believe the bump may have increased its sense of smell, which it probably relied on to find food. It was able to sniff out the best plants or dead animals, whichever it was craving on that particular day.

You know, as Christians, we are supposed to be easy to "sniff out." The Bible says we are to have the aroma of Christ, which means we are supposed to be so much like Jesus that we actually smell like Him. So how do you smell like Jesus? You give off His aroma by being kind to others. You smell like Him by showing love to those around you. When you leave a room, your "Christ perfume" should linger long after you've gone.

So go ahead. Spend time reading God's Word, praying to Him, and sharing His love with others, and you'll be easy to "sniff out" because you'll smell just like Jesus.

**DIGGING DEEPER:**

*Do the people in your life know you're a Christian? How do your words and actions "smell" like Jesus?*

**JURASSIC JOURNALING:**

*Smells always trigger memories. Write about a memory that you have that is attached to a certain smell.*

**DID YOU KNOW** . . . that the Muttaburrasaurus weighed about as much as two black rhinoceroses?

# HYPSILOPHODON
## [hip-sill-OFF-oh-don]

**BIBLE EXCAVATION:**

Know-it-alls don't like being told what to do; they avoid the company of wise men and women.

—PROVERBS 15:12 MSG

## DINO STATS

**FAMILY:**
Hypsilophodontidae

**HEIGHT:**
2 ft. (0.6 m)

**LENGTH:**
6 ft. (1.8 m)

**WEIGHT:**
150 lb. (68 kg)

**DIET:**
plants, possibly insects and small reptiles

## NEVER STOP LEARNING

The Hypsilophodon has been the subject of debate for paleontologists for quite a while. At first, scientists thought this dinosaur perched itself in trees so it could reach leaves too high to get from the ground. But then new evidence was found that totally squashed that theory. Fossils revealed the Hypsilophodon's feet could not grip a branch, so there was no way it could've perched on tree limbs. It would've fallen out! Even though those feet weren't good for tree perching, they were built for fast running. Its slender legs and stiff tail also made this dino quite speedy.

But what if these paleontologists had rejected the new knowledge they'd learned about the Hypsilophodon's feet and never published their new findings? We wouldn't know the latest, greatest information about this dinosaur.

DID YOU KNOW . . . that the Hypsilophodon had a special kind of jaw that moved in such a way it sharpened its upper and lower teeth?

*Think of a time when you thought you were right about something but later found out you were completely wrong. How did it feel to admit you were wrong?*

## JURASSIC JOURNALING:

*Saying you've made a mistake can be tough, but it's easier when you know what to say. Write down an answer you might give your friends when you realize you're wrong about something.*

We should always keep learning and growing. And if we discover we've been wrong about something, we should be quick to admit it and seek the truth in that situation. Proverbs 15:12 says, "Know-it-alls don't like being told what to do; they avoid the company of wise men and women" (MSG). The bottom line? Don't be a know-it-all. Be open to learning something new every day. And be grateful for those who share their wisdom with you.

# PLESIOSAURUS
## [PLEE-see-uh-SORE-us]

**BIBLE EXCAVATION:**

It takes strong winds to move a large sailing ship, but the captain uses only a small rudder to make it go in any direction. Our tongues are small too, and yet they brag about big things.

—JAMES 3:4–5 CEV

## DINO STATS

**FAMILY:**
Plesiosauridae

**HEIGHT:**
3–4 ft. (0.9–1.2 m)

**LENGTH:**
11–16 ft. (3.4–4.9 m)

**WEIGHT:**
200 lb. (90.7 kg)

**DIET:**
meat

# LET GOD STEER YOUR LIFE

The Plesiosaurus, which scientists incorrectly classified as a dinosaur when it was first discovered, was a long-necked reptile that swam very fast by beating its tail from side to side. They've been called the tigers of the oceans. With their strong jaws and sharp teeth, the Plesiosaurus dined on sharks and other tasty creatures of the sea. Paleontologists think this dinosaur-like animal was not only a fast swimmer but also a precise one, using one of its small fins much like the rudder of a ship to steer its large body through the waters. It's interesting that such a small fin could control such a large reptile.

You know, the Bible compares our tongues to the rudder of a ship. Though our tongues are just a small part of our bodies, they have much power. We can use our tongues to say very encouraging words to our family and friends, or we can use those same tongues to say really mean words. The Bible says our words can build people up or tear them down, so let's choose to be encouragers.

Ask God to help control "your rudder" so that you will only say what He wants you to say. If you do that, you'll stay on the right course.

**DIGGING DEEPER:**

*Have you ever totally lost control of "your rudder"? How did that make you feel?*

**JURASSIC JOURNALING:**

*Write five encouraging things you can say to your friends and family this week.*

**DID YOU KNOW . . .** that *Plesiosaurus* means "almost lizard"?

# PTERODAUSTRO
## [terra-DAW-strow]

BIBLE EXCAVATION:

Jesus answered, "It is written: 'Man shall not live on bread alone, but on every word that comes from the mouth of God.'"

—MATTHEW 4:4 NIV

## YOU ARE WHAT YOU EAT

**DINO STATS**

FAMILY:
Ctenochasmatidae

HEIGHT:
4 ft. (1.2 m)

LENGTH:
3–4 ft. (0.9–1.2 m)

WEIGHT:
10 lb. (4.5 kg)

DIET:
shrimp, plankton, small shellfish

With a wingspan of over eight feet, the Pterodaustro was a flying reptile that sort of looked like a cross between a pelican and a flamingo. Scientists think it used its curved beak to scoop up sea water in search of food. Then the Pterodaustro would sift out plankton and other small sea creatures for a meal. It had five hundred pairs of bristle-like teeth in its lower jaw that acted like a filter system.

Because the Pterodaustro ate much of the same things that today's flamingo eats, some scientists believe this bird-like creature was pink since it would've absorbed pink pigment from its food, just as the flamingo does.

Animals aren't the only ones who are greatly affected by what they eat. So are we! You've probably heard the expression "You are what you eat," right? Well, it's true. That's why you learn the importance of eating a balanced diet in health class. If you don't eat healthy foods, you won't have good health.

## DIGGING DEEPER:

*Do you sometimes watch movies you shouldn't watch or listen to music you know you shouldn't listen to? How does that make you feel inside? How do you think it affects you?*

## JURASSIC JOURNALING:

*Write out this scripture to help you memorize it: "Blessed are those who hunger and thirst for righteousness, for they will be filled" (Matthew 5:6 NIV).*

Guess what? It works the same way in our Christian lives. If you aren't eating a steady diet of God's Word every day, you will become spiritually weak and sick. Or if you are eating a lot of "junk food" by watching movies or listening to music your parents don't approve of, your spiritual health will suffer. So eat the good stuff. If you do, you'll be a strong, healthy Christian, and God will be tickled pinker than a Pterodaustro.

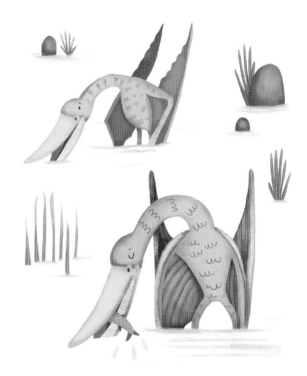

 DID YOU KNOW . . . that the Pterodaustro probably waded on all fours when feeding?

# MAPUSAURUS
## [MAP-oo-SORE-us]

## DINO STATS

**FAMILY:**
Carcharodontosauridae

**HEIGHT:**
13 ft. (4 m)

**LENGTH:**
40–42 ft. (12.2–12.8 m)

**WEIGHT:**
6,600 lb. (2,993.7 kg)

**DIET:**
meat

# WE ARE FAMILY

When paleontologists discovered fossils belonging to the Mapusaurus dinosaurs, they couldn't help but notice how the bones were clustered together. This caused the scientists to believe these dinos were a tight-knit family. With the Mapusaurus bones of babies, teenagers, and adults all found together, it seems these dinos hunted, played, lived, and died as a family unit. Scientists also believe the adult dinos taught their young how to survive in the wild and hunt in a pack. It would've been hard for an individual Mapusaurus to take down a giant Argentinosaurus, but with a pack of Mapusaurus dinos, it was possible.

While it's true that some dinosaurs abandoned their young shortly after they hatched, the Mapusaurus dinos cared for their babies. Can you imagine if we were left to fend for ourselves shortly after birth? That would be tough, wouldn't it? We'd have to learn how to do everything for ourselves from the very beginning. But that's

**DIGGING DEEPER:**

*Do you listen to your parents, grandparents, or older siblings? Or do you have a hard time listening to them and learning from them? If so, why?*

**JURASSIC JOURNALING:**

*Write your family members a short note, thanking each one for making you a better person. For example, you might write, "Thanks, Dad, for helping me with my math homework. I learn so much from you. I love you."*

not how God designed it. He put you in a family with parents and grandparents and maybe even older siblings so that you could learn, grow, and thrive! Make sure you learn all you can from those who are older than you—especially your parents—so when it's your time to go out on your own, you'll be ready. Show them respect and gratitude, and cherish your pack. Why not take a moment and thank God for your family right now?

**DID YOU KNOW** . . . that *Mapusaurus* means "earth lizard"?

# COMPSOGNATHUS
## [comp-sog-NAYTH-us]

BIBLE EXCAVATION:

Pride goes before destruction, a haughty spirit before a fall.

—PROVERBS 16:18 NIV

## DID SOMEBODY ASK FOR HELP?

**DINO STATS**

**FAMILY:**
Compsognathidae

**HEIGHT:**
10 in. (0.3 m)
at the hips

**LENGTH:**
3 ft. (0.9 m)

**WEIGHT:**
6.5 lb. (2.9 kg)

**DIET:**
mostly insects,
spiders, worms,
small lizards

Only the size of a chicken, this little dinosaur was speedy! Paleontologists think the Compsognathus could run as fast as 40 miles per hour. It had long legs, claws, and sharp little teeth. Almost everything about it was little.

While this dinosaur chased after small prey, sometimes it would watch and wait for a free meal. Because it was so small, the Compsognathus let the more powerful predators kill unsuspecting dinos, and then the Compsognathus would sneak in and snack on the dead animals much like a vulture. While this might seem gross, it was pretty smart because this dino was too small to kill the larger dinos on its own, so it let the bigger predators do that instead.

It's not that this little dino was being lazy; it was just being smart. We can learn from the Compsognathus by playing it smart and allowing those who have strengths that we don't have to help us whenever we need assistance. Why wouldn't we let others help us when we are unable to do something for ourselves?

Pride. That's what keeps us from receiving help

Do you have a hard time asking for help and receiving help? Why?

Write about a time when you were too proud to ask for help. What other emotions did you feel besides pride? Were you embarrassed? Angry? Nervous?

from others. But you know what the Bible says about pride? It says that pride comes before a fall, meaning you shouldn't rely only on yourself when you know you need help. To stop the "I can do it myself" attitude, accept help when you need it. That's the smart thing to do.

 DID YOU KNOW . . . that the tail makes up half the length of the Compsognathus?

# OVIRAPTOR
[OH-vih-RAP-tore]

**BIBLE EXCAVATION:**

Let us not grow weary of doing good, for in due season we will reap, if we do not give up.

—GALATIANS 6:9 ESV

## DINO STATS

**FAMILY:**
Oviraptoridae

**HEIGHT:**
3–5 ft. (0.9–1.5 m)

**LENGTH:**
8 ft. (2.4 m)

**WEIGHT:**
45 lb. (20.4 kg)

**DIET:**
reptiles, nuts, fruits

**DID YOU KNOW** . . . that a female dinosaur laid anywhere from three to twenty eggs at a time?

# IN DUE SEASON

In the early 1990s, paleontologists discovered the fossil of an Oviraptor **brooding** her egg-filled nest in the Gobi Desert. It seems she died protecting her eggs. That dinosaur fossil became known as "Big Mama." It was one of the most important dinosaur fossils ever discovered because it proved that dinos sat on their eggs much like birds. They would sit on their eggs to keep them warm and protect them from predators so the baby dinosaurs would hatch at just the right time.

The Bible calls a time when something is supposed to happen a "due season." Galatians 6:9 says, "Let us not grow weary of doing good, for in due season we will reap, if we do not give up" (ESV). You see, if the baby dinosaurs had been born too soon, they wouldn't have been healthy, and many would've died. It's the same way with our dreams. If we give birth to our dreams too soon—before they are "due"—they might die before they have a fighting chance.

The Bible tells us that everything under heaven has a set time, and even though we tend to be impatient, it's much better if we trust God to deliver our dreams at their "set time." That doesn't mean we should just wait around and do nothing during the incubation time. We should prepare to walk in our dreams without trying to "give birth" to them before their due season. Ask God to help you be patient as you follow the path He has for your life, and ask Him to help you never miss a "due season."

## DIGGING DEEPER:

Do you get impatient waiting on dreams to come true? What can you do in the meantime?

## JURASSIC JOURNALING:

Describe a dream that you'd love to see come true in your life—a dream that you feel God has placed inside you. Now, write "Due Season" over the top it.

## DINO DICTIONARY:

**brooding**—when egg-laying animals sit on their eggs, keeping them warm with their body heat until they are ready to be hatched.

# ARGENTINOSAURUS
## [ar-jen-TEEN-oh-SORE-us]

**BIBLE EXCAVATION:**

Neither the one who plants nor the one who waters
is anything, but only God, who makes things grow.

—1 CORINTHIANS 3:7 NIV

## DINO STATS

**FAMILY:**
Titanosauridae

**HEIGHT:**
70 ft. (21.3 m)

**LENGTH:**
70–115 ft.
(21.3–35.1 m)

**WEIGHT:**
150,000–160,000
lb. (68,038.9–
72,574.8 kg)

**DIET:**
plants

## SLOW GROWING

Weighing as much as ten African elephants, the Argentinosaurus was a gigantic plant-eating dinosaur—one of the largest dinosaurs to have ever lived. It's hard to believe this enormous dinosaur came from an egg the size of a beach ball. If that's true, the baby dino would have to have grown 25,000 times its original size before becoming full-grown. Some scientists believe it would have taken fifteen years for this slow-growing dinosaur to reach its adult size.

You see, some things take a long time to grow, but they are totally worth the wait. It makes sense that the Argentinosaurus would've taken longer than other dinos to grow into its adult size—it was one of the biggest creatures ever!

One day you may be a spiritual giant—a person who will do impressive things for God and make an

DID YOU KNOW . . . that the Argentinosaurus
was almost as long as a football field is wide?

**DIGGING DEEPER:**

*Do you ever feel like everyone in your life is more mature than you are? How do you think God could use you to do big things?*

**JURASSIC JOURNALING:**

*Write five things that take a while to mature but are totally worth the wait. For example, a baby takes nine months to grow inside a mother's tummy.*

enormous impact for heaven. But perhaps you're not quite ready yet. God is growing you up—inside and out—to mature you into the person He can use to change the world. And you can help in that process by spending time praying, reading the Bible, memorizing scriptures, and going to church. And just singing praises to God is a great way to grow. You may be slow-growing now, but take heart! God is taking His time with you, and that's a gigantic blessing.

# SARMIENTOSAURUS
[SAR-mee-en-toe-SORE-us]

BIBLE EXCAVATION:

Open my eyes that I may see wonderful things in your law.

—PSALM 119:18 NIV

## DINO STATS

**FAMILY:**
Titanosauridae

**HEIGHT:**
Unknown

**LENGTH:**
40 ft. (12.2 m)

**WEIGHT:**
22,000 lb.
(9,979 kg)

**DIET:**
plants

# HOW'S YOUR EYESIGHT?

Scientists have found various fossils of the Sarmientosaurus, but all the bones have been parts of that dino's head and neck—not one bone from the rest of the body. Still, from the bones they have recovered, scientists are sure that this dino was quite big. Using **CT scans**, scientists have also determined that while the Sarmientosaurus had a small brain, it had very large eyeballs, meaning it had great eyesight. In fact, it had much better vision than other Titanosaurs. The Sarmientosaurus could probably have seen predators far off, giving it a chance to get away. You might say this dino's eyesight was a great help to it.

Good eyesight is a gift, don't you think? It allows us to see clearly the world around us.

It works the same way with our spiritual eyesight. We are either spiritually blind or spiritually observant. If we are spiritually blind, we are not able to see God clearly or understand His ways or His Word. But if we are spiritually observant, we will be able to see the world through God's eyes. We will understand what we read in the Bible and know how to apply it to our lives. Having good spiritual eyesight is even more important than having good physical eyesight. So, how's your eyesight? Ask God to help you see and understand new truths in the Bible.

DID YOU KNOW . . . that some scientists believe the Sarmientosaurus walked with its nose pointing down so it could nibble on low-growing plants?

# AMARGASAURUS
## [ah-MARG-uh-SORE-us]

## DON'T BE A HOT HEAD!

### DINO STATS

**FAMILY:**
Dicraeosauridae

**HEIGHT:**
4–10 ft. (1.2–3 m)

**LENGTH:**
30–33 ft.
(9.1–10.1 m)

**WEIGHT:**
10,000–14,000
lb. (4,535.9–
6,350.3 kg)

**DIET:**
plants

The Amargasaurus had pairs of large rods sticking out of its spine—the biggest rods were about six feet tall! Scientists are still unsure what the strange rods were used for, but they have some theories. Some think when the Amargasaurus shook its neck, the rods would clang into each other and make a loud noise, which could've been used to scare off predators. But a more popular theory is that those rods supported a large sail on this dino's back—a sail that was used to regulate the dino's temperature. Since the Amargasaurus lived in a dry, hot environment, scientists believe it might've used these sails to cool off when it became overheated, much like an elephant uses its large ears.

Sometimes we all need to cool off, don't we? And I'm not talking about being hot; I'm talking about being a hothead. It's not a sin to get angry, but it's a sin to stay that way. A lot of situations in life will make you mad. You can't always control those situations, but you can control how

*Part of dealing with anger is figuring out why you're mad. Did someone embarrass you? Were you harmed in some way? Get to the root of your anger by talking with a trusted adult—a parent, a teacher, a pastor, or even a counselor.*

## JURASSIC JOURNALING:

*Write about the last time you got really angry. Did you handle it well? Were you mad for a long time? Are you still angry?*

you react. The Bible tells us not to sin in our anger. It also says, "Do not let the sun go down while you are still angry" (Ephesians 4:26 NIV). Use this opportunity to practice one of the fruits of the Spirit—self-control! Ask God to help you deal with your anger. Staying mad isn't good for you or anyone around you, so take it from the Amargasaurus and find a way to cool off.

 **DID YOU KNOW** . . . that the Amargasaurus weighed about as much as two white rhinoceroses?

# IGUANODON
## [ig-WAH-na-DON]

BIBLE EXCAVATION:

Not that I have already obtained it or have already
become perfect, but I press on so that I may lay hold of
that for which also I was laid hold of by Christ Jesus.

—PHILIPPIANS 3:12 NASB

## DINO STATS

**FAMILY:**
Iguanodontidae

**HEIGHT:**
16 ft. (4.9 m)

**LENGTH:**
33–39 ft.
(10.1–11.9 m)

**WEIGHT:**
10,000 lb.
(4,535.9 kg)

**DIET:**
plants

# PROGRESS, NOT PERFECTION

Paleontologists, like everyone else in the world, are not perfect. They, too, make mistakes. Gideon Mantell, a famous paleontologist in the 1800s, put an Iguanodon's thumb claw on top of its nose. And it stayed that way for forty years! Another paleontologist in the 1800s, Edward Cope, reconstructed an Elasmosaurus with its head on the end of its tail! And until just recently, the Apatosaurus was shown in museums with the head of a Camarasaurus. Oops!

Nobody is perfect except for God, and mistakes are just the pebbles on the path to success. Don't beat yourself up about not being perfect. Instead, adopt this healthy attitude: progress, not perfection. Every mistake you make just puts you one step closer to getting it right, so don't stress over being imperfect. Don't expect perfection from yourself or the people in your life. Remember, our true perfection will only come when we get to heaven.

**DIGGING DEEPER:**

*Why do you strive to be perfect? Do you feel that your parents expect perfection? Your teachers? Coaches? Do you expect perfection of yourself?*

**JURASSIC JOURNALING:**

*Write about a mistake you made and the lesson you learned from that mistake.*

Be kind to yourself and others when you make big mistakes. Learn to laugh at yourself and simply try again. If you can do that, you'll enjoy life so much more. And you'll be more willing to take risks and do hard things because you won't fear failure. You'll go for it, knowing that perfection isn't a reality and moving toward perfection is progress.

**DID YOU KNOW** . . . that the Iguanodon was the first creature to be scientifically recognized as a dinosaur?

# DREADNOUGHTUS
## [dred-NAWT-us]

**BIBLE EXCAVATION:**

"Everyone who hears these words of mine and does not do them will be like a foolish man who built his house on the sand. And the rain fell, and the floods came, and the winds blew and beat against that house, and it fell, and great was the fall of it."

—MATTHEW 7:26–27 ESV

## SINKING SAND

DINO STATS

**FAMILY:**
Titanosauridae

**HEIGHT:**
20 ft. (6.1 m)

**LENGTH:**
85 ft. (25.9 m)

**WEIGHT:**
130,000 lb.
(58,967 kg)

**DIET:**
plants

The Dreadnoughtus was one of the biggest dinosaurs to walk the earth. In fact, this huge dino was named after a battleship because of its enormity and power. When paleontologist Kenneth Lacovara found a leg bone in Argentina, he had no idea what an amazing find he was about to uncover. It took him and his fellow scientists four summers to collect all of this dinosaur's fossils, which was about 70 percent of a complete skeleton. And that ended up being the most complete Sauropod skeleton ever found!

Scientists say this large-and-in-charge dinosaur could've simply leaned on a T. Rex to kill it, but it couldn't take on a raging river. Their theory is that a flooded river probably drowned this gigantic dinosaur and then swept it onto a bed of quicksand, which swallowed the dinosaur whole! That's the reason the bones were so beautifully preserved. Bad luck for the dinosaur, but great luck for the scientists.

Quicksand is dangerous stuff. Maybe that's why

*How are you following after Jesus and building your life on the solid Rock?*

*The story Jesus shared about building a house on sinking sand or solid ground is called a parable. A parable is when you use a story to teach something. Try writing your own parable.*

Jesus used sand to explain how a wise person builds his house on solid rock but a fool builds his house on sinking sand. Jesus shared this story to show we need to build our lives on Him and His way of life. If we build our lives on anything else, we will be building it on sinking sand—and we know how dangerous that sand can be. Just ask the Dreadnoughtus. So let's build our lives on solid ground. Let's build our lives on Jesus.

 DID YOU KNOW . . . that *Dreadnoughtus* means "fear nothing"?

# ALLOSAURUS
## [AL-oh-SORE-us]

We can make our plans, but the LORD determines our steps.

— PROVERBS 16:9 NLT

## DINO STATS

**FAMILY:**
Allosauridae

**HEIGHT:**
10–17 ft. (3–5.2 m)

**LENGTH:**
30–40 ft.
(9.1–12.2 m)

**WEIGHT:**
2,000–8,000 lb.
(907.2–3,628.7 kg)

**DIET:**
meat

**DID YOU KNOW** . . . that a teenage Allosaurus—almost a complete fossil—was discovered in Wyoming in 1991 and named "Big Al"?

# MAKE AN IMPACT

When the local coal miners in Elk Valley, British Columbia, found a large piece of rock with footprints from at least three different kinds of dinosaurs, paleontologists all over the world got excited. This was big news! The footprints included large imprints from a big meat-eating dinosaur that they think was an Allosaurus, some rounded prints that most likely came from a long-necked Sauropod, and prints from a smaller dinosaur that is yet to be determined.

This find was so important because the footprints, known as a *trackway*, show actual activity of the animals where they dwelled, unlike other fossils that are often found very far from where the dinos lived and died. It seems that footprints tell us a lot—what kind of dinosaur it was, how it lived, how it hunted and traveled, how big it grew, and more.

Because footprints reveal so much, let me ask you this: What story would your footprints tell? What kind of impact are you making in your family, school, and neighborhood? If you're worried that your story wouldn't be a very good one, then it's time to change your footprints. It's time to let Jesus lead you and to follow His plan for your life. That way, your impact will be huge—even bigger than the footprint of an Allosaurus!

**DIGGING DEEPER:**

*Have you ever wondered how you'll be remembered? What kind of footprints have you left behind so far?*

**JURASSIC JOURNALING:**

*Trace one of your feet and write this: "What footprint will I leave today?" That will be a good reminder for you to make an impact every day.*

# LEAELLYNASAURA
## [lee-EL-in-ah-SORE-a]

**BIBLE EXCAVATION:**

"I, yes, I, am the one who comforts you. So why are you afraid of mere humans, who wither like the grass and disappear?"

—ISAIAH 51:12 NLT

## DINO STATS

**FAMILY:**
Hypsilophodontidae

**HEIGHT:**
16 in. (0.4 m)

**LENGTH:**
3 ft. (0.9 m)

**WEIGHT:**
6–22 lb. (2.7–10 kg)

**DIET:**
plants

## A LITTLE COMFORT

The Leaellynasaura lived in a region that had seasons of almost total darkness and freezing conditions. So it may have been a chilly dino, but it was super cute! It had very large eyes, which helped it see in low-light conditions. Experts think the Leaellynasaura probably **burrowed** into the ground to protect itself from the harsh, cold weather and possibly hibernated during the worst weather months. Fossils also show that this tiny dinosaur was mostly tail. In fact, scientists estimate that its tail made up almost 75 percent of its total body length. And much like a squirrel, the Leaellynasaura might have used its long, furry tail to keep warm, wrapping itself in it for comfort.

We all need a little comfort sometimes, don't we? Did you have a special blanket you slept with when you were younger? Or maybe you had a favorite stuffed

**DID YOU KNOW . . .** that *Leaellynasaura* was named after the paleontologists' daughter who always wanted her own dinosaur?

animal that kept you company when you went to bed. Those are comfort items. They make us feel secure and peaceful at night. Well, you may have given up your blankie and your stuffed animal and you probably don't have a bushy tail, but you do have the best comforter of all—God!

Psalm 119:76 says, "May your unfailing love be my comfort" (NIV). Just picture His love wrapped around you like your favorite blanket. God promises to never leave you (Hebrews 13:5) and to give you sweet sleep (Proverbs 3:24). So if you feel worried at night, just thank Him for giving you comfort, peace, and sweet sleep, and then rest in Him.

# HUALIANCERATOPS
## [who-lee-on-SERR-a-TOPS]

**BIBLE EXCAVATION:**

Who can measure the wealth and wisdom and knowledge of God?

—ROMANS 11:33 CEV

## DINO STATS

**FAMILY:**
Chaoyangsauridae

**HEIGHT:**
1–2 ft. (0.3–0.6 m)

**LENGTH:**
5 ft. (1.5 m)

**WEIGHT:**
30–45 lb.
(13.6–20.4 kg)

**DIET:**
plants

 **DID YOU KNOW . . .** that *Hualianceratops* most likely walked on two legs, not four?

# GOD KNOWS IT ALL

In 2015, when researchers discovered a partial skull and foot of the Hualianceratops in China, it was a big deal. Here's why: finding this new species in the same fossil bed with other Ceratopsians revealed there was quite a bit more **diversity** than originally thought. The Hualianceratops, which was about the size of a medium-size dog, didn't have horns like its cousin the Triceratops (which was found in the same area in 2002), and it wasn't nearly as big. The Triceratops was 30 feet long and weighed about 20,000 pounds!

Scientists are learning things all the time. Early on, they didn't think each family of dinosaurs could be so varied. But after the discovery of the Hualianceratops, they realized there is much more to learn about the way dinosaurs lived and developed.

Paleontologists are some pretty smart people, but they don't know everything. No matter how much we know or think we know, we can always learn something new. That's why we should keep seeking knowledge and always be open to new ideas. And we should remember to turn to God, the knower of all things, for insight and wisdom. Don't forget to include Him in your search for knowledge. Ask Him to help you remember what you study. Ask Him to open your eyes to new information. God can give you spiritual knowledge through the Holy Spirit that lives inside you, and then you'll make better decisions—both big and small.

# EOLAMBIA
## [EE-oh-LAM-bee-ah]

**BIBLE EXCAVATION:**

God has placed the parts in the body, every one of them, just as he wanted them to be. If they were all one part, where would the body be? As it is, there are many parts, but one body.

—1 CORINTHIANS 12:18–20 NIV

## EVERYONE IS IMPORTANT

**DINO STATS**

**FAMILY:**
Hadrosauroidea

**HEIGHT:**
6–7 ft. (1.8–2.1 m)

**LENGTH:**
20–30 ft.
(6.1–9.1 m)

**WEIGHT:**
2,200 lb. (997.9 kg)

**DIET:**
plants

The first fossil remains of an Eolambia dinosaur were found in Utah in 1992. It was just one of several Ornithopods discovered in this quarry in Utah. Someone once described them as "not too bright and smallish." (Not exactly the kind of description you'd want, huh?) There was nothing super special about the Eolambia. It had a stiff tail and spikes on its thumbs, and it was larger than some of the other plant-eating dinos at that time, but still they were easy targets for Raptors and Tyrannosaurs. All in all, Eolambias were pretty ordinary dinosaurs, but there were a lot of them, and they were essential to their ecosystem. If it hadn't been for them, the Tyrannosaurs wouldn't have survived because the Eolambias were an essential food source!

Ever felt like an ordinary dino? God must've known we'd all feel insignificant at some point because He talks about this issue in 1 Corinthians 12. That passage talks about how every part of the human body is essential. Just think about it—if the ears decided they wanted to be eyes,

JURASSIC JOURNALING:

*Write about a time when you wanted to be "an ear" instead of "an eye." Have you ever wished the role you play were different?*

we'd have four eyes and no hearing! (We'd look pretty silly too.) We need our ears and our eyes. They do different things, but they're equally important. And so are we. Whether you're "an eye" or "an ear" in the kingdom of God, you are essential.

**DID YOU KNOW** . . . that the Eolambia was the earliest-known duckbill?

# KUNBARRASAURUS
## [KOON-ba-rah-SORE-us]

BIBLE EXCAVATION:

We also pray that you will be strengthened with all his glorious power so you will have all the endurance and patience you need. May you be filled with joy.

—COLOSSIANS 1:11 NLT

## YOU'RE STRONGER THAN YOU THINK

**DINO STATS**

**FAMILY:**
Ankylosauridae

**HEIGHT:**
Unknown

**LENGTH:**
6–10 ft. (1.8–3 m)

**WEIGHT:**
550 lb. (249.5 kg)

**DIET:**
plants

A well-preserved fossil skeleton of the Kunbarrasaurus was discovered in Australia in 1989, and scientists considered it quite a find. (Some of its stomach contents were still preserved!) Because it was so well-kept, we know a bit about this dinosaur's life. Scientists say the Kunbarrasaurus was slow-moving and probably not very smart. It was about the size of a sheep and had less armor than other Ankylosaurs, but it did have spikes sticking out from its hips and armored plates covering its tail. And here's something super interesting about this dino—the Kunbarrasaurus had stomach armor that grew underneath its skin! It was like hidden armor on the inside of its belly!

Just looking at this dinosaur, you wouldn't have been able to tell it had armor protecting its stomach. But the armor was there—it was just hidden. In other words, this dinosaur was even tougher than it looked! And you know what? So are you!

People can't see what's on the inside of you, but that doesn't matter, because you know God has put strength, **perseverance**, and courage inside you. It's your inner armor! You can go through any hurt, any hardship, and any kind of trouble and still be standing. It doesn't matter if life punches you right in the gut—with God's help, you're strong enough to withstand it. That doesn't mean life won't hurt sometimes, but it means you'll survive and will have an encouraging story to share with others.

So stand strong! Be brave! You have hidden strength that may surprise you.

DIGGING DEEPER:

*Do you feel strong? Do you feel brave? If not, ask God to help you feel and see the inner armor He gives you.*

JURASSIC JOURNALING:

*The name Kunbarrasaurus means "shield lizard," which is fitting since this dino was heavily armored. What words would someone use to best describe you? Write them in your journal.*

DINO DICTIONARY:

*perseverance—doing something no matter how difficult it is or how long it takes.*

DID YOU KNOW . . . that the Kunbarrasaurus had an inner ear system much larger than most dinosaurs?

# CORYTHOSAURUS
## [ko-RITH-o-SORE-us]

"My sheep hear my voice, and I know them, and they follow me."

—JOHN 10:27 ESV

## CAN YOU HEAR HIM NOW?

### DINO STATS

**FAMILY:**
Lambeosaurinae

**HEIGHT:**
6–7 ft. (1.8–2.1 m)

**LENGTH:**
30–33 ft.
(9.1–10.1 m)

**WEIGHT:**
8,000–10,000
lb. (3,628.7–
4,535.9 kg)

**DIET:**
plants

This dinosaur had a hollow, bony crest on top of its long head, which sort of looked like a helmet. Scientists think this duck-billed dino walked and ran on two legs. And apparently, it could run fast and go far, which is a good thing since experts also think the Corythosaurus ran away from danger instead of sticking around to fight.

Luckily for this dinosaur, the Corythosaurus had exceptional eyesight and hearing, so it knew when predators were coming its way, giving it plenty of time to get away. In fact, after running several tests, scientists now believe the Corythosaurus had a special inner ear that enabled it to hear **low-frequency** sounds from far away. That great sense of hearing probably saved this dinosaur's life many times.

Good hearing could save your life too, especially if you're tuned in to God's voice. The Bible says Jesus is the Good Shepherd and we're His sheep. It also says sheep know their shepherd's voice and listen to that

DIGGING DEEPER:

Do you hear God's voice? Think of a time when you knew you'd heard from Him. How did you respond to Him?

JURASSIC JOURNALING:

Paleontologist Barnum Brown named the Corythosaurus in 1914. He thought their heads looked like the helmets worn by soldiers of Corinth, so he named it Corythosaurus, which meant "Corinthian helmet lizard." If you were able to name this lizard, what names would you have chosen?

DINO DICTIONARY:

**low frequency**—a sound that is lower than 20 cycles per second, the normal limit of human hearing.

voice above all other voices and sounds. That's how we should be living—listening to God and tuning out all competing voices.

Now, I'm not talking about hearing God's voice like a big, deep *boom* coming from the sky. It's not like that. When God speaks to us, it's more of a whisper deep down in our hearts. As you spend time reading His Word and praying, you'll begin to know His voice, and you'll be able to hear it over all the other noises in your life. So tune in to Jesus today. It's the only way to live.

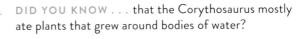

DID YOU KNOW . . . that the Corythosaurus mostly ate plants that grew around bodies of water?

# MAMENCHISAURUS
## [mah–MEHN–chee–SORE–us]

**BIBLE EXCAVATION:**

"If you sinful people know how to give good gifts to your children, how much more will your heavenly Father give good gifts to those who ask him."

—MATTHEW 7:11 NLT

## DINO STATS

**FAMILY:**
Mamenchisauridae

**HEIGHT:**
26–35 ft.
(7.9–10.7 m)

**LENGTH:**
80–115 ft.
(24.4–35.1 m)

**WEIGHT:**
30,000–60,000 lb. (13,607.8–27,215.5 kg)

**DIET:**
plants

# UNEXPECTED BLESSINGS

The Mamenchisaurus may have had the longest neck of any dinosaur in the history of the world. In fact, its neck was as long as the rest of its body, including its tail! It was such a large dinosaur that it might not have needed too many defenses to survive, which is a good thing because the Mamenchisaurus didn't have many. It certainly couldn't move very fast to outrun predators. And it didn't have any spikes or claws to use as weapons, although it might've had a club-like tail.

Did you know this dino wasn't discovered by paleontologists who were out on a dig? Nope, it was found by workers who were building a bridge in central China. What a fun surprise for those workers!

You know, God likes to surprise us too. He may not leave dinosaur bones around every corner for you to discover, but every day with Him is a new adventure. He knows your favorite things and how to brighten your day. Look for His surprises in the simple things, like when a butterfly lands on your hand or when you see a rainbow and it hasn't been raining. God loves to give, so expect to see His gifts every day. And be sure to thank Him when you experience one of those God surprises.

**DIGGING DEEPER:**

*When have you experienced a God surprise? Did you take time to thank Him for it?*

**JURASSIC JOURNALING:**

*Wouldn't it be fun to let God use you to surprise someone in your life with something special? Write down the names of a few people and then write their favorite things next to their name. Now, try to bless each of those people with a surprise sometime soon.*

 **DID YOU KNOW** . . . that the Mamenchisaurus's head was smaller than a horse's head on a body longer than two school buses?

# FALCARIUS
[fal-cuh-RYE-us]

**BIBLE EXCAVATION:**

"If you lived on the world's terms, the world would love you as one of its own. But since I picked you to live on God's terms and no longer on the world's terms, the world is going to hate you."

—JOHN 15:19 MSG

## YOU DON'T HAVE TO FIT IN

**DINO STATS**

**FAMILY:**
Therizinosauria

**HEIGHT:**
4 ft. (1.2 m)

**LENGTH:**
12 ft. (3.7 m)

**WEIGHT:**
450–650 lb.
(204.1–294.8 kg)

**DIET:**
plants

The Falcarius had a very long neck, a long tail, and odd **sickle claws**. These claws seemed out of place on this dino because usually only meat-eaters had claws like that, and it was determined the Falcarius was a plant-eater. Not only that, the Falcarius was a Theropod, belonging to the Therizinosauroid group, and most Theropods were meat-eaters. In addition, most Therizinosauroids were sloth-like dinosaurs—slow and awkward. But the Falcarius had long legs and a skinny tail, leading scientists to believe it was a fast runner. It would seem the Falcarius wasn't like any other dino relatives.

It's okay to be different. Throughout history, we have examples of people doing amazing things, and they almost always didn't fit in with their peers. For example, take English paleontologist Mary Anning. She lived in the 1800s when women weren't respected as much as they are today. Most women and girls didn't

**DID YOU KNOW . . .** that the Falcarius's sickle claws were about 10 centimeters long?

DIGGING DEEPER:

*Have you ever wished you could fit in better with your friends? Do you always feel like you're the odd one in your group? How does that make you feel?*

JURASSIC JOURNALING:

*Write about a time when you felt really alone because you were the only person in your group who believed a certain way.*

DINO DICTIONARY:

**sickle claw**—*a curved claw.*

receive formal education, but Mary did. She was very bright and quite driven. She found her first dinosaur skeleton at age twelve! Scientists of the day didn't know what to do with Mary. She was a woman and came from a poor family. Most scientists at that time were men from wealthy families. So she wasn't taken as seriously as she should've been, but she contributed greatly to the study of dinosaurs in her forty-seven years.

So go ahead—be different! Push the limits. Follow the path God has for you, no matter how different it may be from your friends' paths. You were born to stand out. You were born to do great things. You were born for such a time as this.

# OPISTHOCOELICAUDIA
## [Oh-PIS-tho-SEEL-ih-CAWD-ee-ah]

**BIBLE EXCAVATION:**

Let's walk right up to him and get what he is so
ready to give. Take the mercy, accept the help.

—HEBREWS 4:16 MSG

## DINO STATS

**FAMILY:**
Saltasauridae

**HEIGHT:**
16 ft. (4.9 m)

**LENGTH:**
36–40 ft.
(11–12.2 m)

**WEIGHT:**
40,000 lb.
(18,143.7 kg)

**DIET:**
plants

**DID YOU KNOW** . . . that the name
*Opisthocoelicaudia* means "hollow-backed tail"?

# A LITTLE SUPPORT

A skeleton of the Opisthocoelicaudia was discovered in the Gobi Desert, but it was missing the dino's head and neck. So we can't be sure exactly how the Opisthocoelicaudia looked, but scientists think it was a shorter, heavier version of other Sauropods with a small head sitting on top of a long neck.

The Opisthocoelicaudia was a plant-eater, and in order to reach leaves high up in the trees, it had to use its tail as a sort of a third leg for support. It had a very specialized tail designed for strength and support.

We all need a little support sometimes, don't we? For the Opisthocoelicaudias, its tail support helped it survive. If it couldn't balance itself long enough to feed on the tender leaves (and lots of them), it would've died.

What about you? Don't you need support sometimes, not only physically but also emotionally and spiritually? Whether you're feeling a little down or totally overwhelmed, isn't it nice to have the support of your friends and family to get you through? We all need that special group of loved ones to cheer us up. Maybe you don't feel like you have anyone in your life to encourage and support you, but you do. God is your biggest supporter. You can trust Him. The Bible says all you have to do is call on Him, and He is ready, willing, and able to help you in every situation. So don't try to go it alone. Call on your heavenly Father, your biggest supporter.

## DIGGING DEEPER:

*Who supports you? Your parents and friends? Maybe your school counselor or pastor has been there for you when you needed it. Remember, no matter what, you always have God in your corner.*

## JURASSIC JOURNALING:

*Support can come in many different ways. One way you could support others is through encouragement. Maybe you could write thank-you letters to veterans living in your city. Ask your parents for help locating these brave men and women.*

# SPINOPS STERNBERGORUM
## [SPIN-ops stern-berg-OR-uhm]

BIBLE EXCAVATION:

For am I now seeking the approval of man, or of God? Or am I trying to please man? If I were still trying to please man, I would not be a servant of Christ.

—GALATIANS 1:10 ESV

## YOU'RE ALREADY APPROVED

### DINO STATS

**FAMILY:**
Ceratopsidae

**HEIGHT:**
Unknown

**LENGTH:**
20 ft. (6.1 m)

**WEIGHT:**
4,000 lb.
(1,814.4 kg)

**DIET:**
plants

Fossil collectors Charles H. Sternberg and his son Levi found several parts of a dinosaur's skull—part of a nasal horn, eye sockets, parts of the frill, and little brow horns—but the upper and lower jaws were missing. Still, this father-and-son team knew they had found something special. They thought they may have found a new dinosaur that's related to the Styracosaurus.

The Sternbergs sent their findings to London's Natural History Museum, thinking the scientists at the museum would be equally excited. Instead, museum paleontologist Arthur Smith Woodward wrote a letter to them, saying their find was "nothing but rubbish." So all those precious fossils were put on a shelf—for ninety years!

In 2004, a scientist looking through the museum's collections found those dusty old bones the Sternbergs had sent. He saw their value, and after he and his fellow scientists studied them, they found out the Sternbergs had been right all along. The dinosaur they found was closely related to the Styracosaurus, but it was an entirely new dinosaur!

DIGGING DEEPER:

*Have you ever tried to share your faith with others? If so, how did that go?*

JURASSIC JOURNALING:

*Pretend you've just found dinosaur fossils in your backyard. Describe what you think the dinosaur would have been like and give it a name.*

They named it *Spinops Sternbergorum* because of its spiny-looking face and to honor the Sternberg family.

So here's the deal—not everyone is going to celebrate what you do or even agree with you. But that's okay. You just keep on "sharing your findings"—witnessing to people about God in a loving way—and don't worry that some may react negatively. We aim for God's approval, not humanity's. God sees your good work, and that's all that matters.

 **DID YOU KNOW** . . . that there are more dinosaurs that haven't been discovered yet than there are paleontologists?

# XENOCERATOPS
## [ZEE-noe-SEH-rah-tops]

# THE FORGOTTEN DINO

**DINO STATS**

**FAMILY:**
Ceratopsidae

**HEIGHT:**
10 ft. (3 m)

**LENGTH:**
20 ft. (6.1 m)

**WEIGHT:**
4,000 lb.
(1,814.4 kg)

**DIET:**
plants

In 1958, paleontologist Wann Langston Jr. found pieces of three dinosaur skulls in a rock formation in Alberta, Canada, and he was less than excited. You see, Langston was busy working on other digs, so he stuck these fossils in a drawer at the Canadian Museum of Nature—and forgot about them!

In 2003, paleontologist David Evans and his colleagues found out about the forgotten fossils and tried to use them to fill in fossil gaps for other dinosaur skeletons. But as they studied the skull fragments, they soon realized those skull pieces belonged to a new type of horned dinosaur—the Xenoceratops.

Nobody likes to be forgotten—not even a dinosaur. Isn't it good to know that God, the Creator of the universe, will never forget you? You are always on His mind. Psalm 139:17–18 says, "How precious are your thoughts about me, O God. They cannot be numbered! I can't even count them; they outnumber the grains of sand!" (NLT). He is thinking about you all the time, so He

**DIGGING DEEPER:**

*Sometimes it's easy to forget about God because you can't actually see Him. But you can see Him through reading His Word. What are some other ways you can better remember God this week?*

**JURASSIC JOURNALING:**

*What do you think makes a person memorable? What makes you memorable? Write your answers.*

could never forget you. But do you ever forget God? Do you put off your time reading His Word and praying to Him? You shouldn't! The more time you spend in God's presence, the more amazing you'll become as He transforms you into the person He has called you to be. And *that* person? That person is very memorable.

 **DID YOU KNOW** . . . that *Xenoceratops* means "alien horned-face"?

# PINACOSAURUS
## [PIN-ah-co-SORE-us]

Friends come and friends go, but a true friend sticks by you like family.

—PROVERBS 18:24 MSG

## PEOPLE CHANGE, GOD DOES NOT

**DINO STATS**

**FAMILY:**
Ankylosauridae

**HEIGHT:**
2–4 ft. (0.6–1.2 m)

**LENGTH:**
16–18 ft.
(4.9–5.5 m)

**WEIGHT:**
2,200–6,600 lb.
(997.9–2,993.7 kg)

**DIET:**
plants

The Pinacosaurus was a rather average-size dinosaur, but it had some pretty intense armor with rows of spikes from its neck to its tail. Over the years, scientists have found lots of Pinacosaurus dinosaurs fossilized together. This leads them to believe this dino was very social—at least for a season.

Some experts who have studied the Pinacosaurus suggest this kind of dino lived in group settings while they were young but most likely left the group and lived alone once they were older. In other words, they ditched all their friends and family after they got older.

What about you? Have you ever been ditched? Friendship can be a funny thing. You may think your BFF will really be your best friend *forever* . . . until she moves away. Long-distance friendships are hard to keep up, so you and your BFF may grow apart until suddenly you're not close anymore. It happens.

But here's the good news! The Bible says that God is a friend who sticks closer than a brother (Proverbs 18:24), and He doesn't change. That means He will

DIGGING DEEPER:

What are some ways
you can become a
better friend?

JURASSIC
JOURNALING:

Write the names of
friends you were super
close with once but now
you're not. Can those
friendships be restored? If
you want to rebuild your
friendships, make the first
step today and reach out
to those past friends. Ask
God to help you.

forever be your best friend. He will be there
for you in good times and bad times. You can
talk to Him about anything. And even when
you act ugly, He still loves you. God is the best
example of how to be a best friend. So imitate
Him, and you'll be the kind of friend someone
would like to have.

 DID YOU KNOW . . . that *Pinacosaurus* means "plank lizard"?

# DUBREUILLOSAURUS
## [du-BROY-oh-SORE-us]

GOD, pick up the pieces. Put me back together again. You are my praise!

—JEREMIAH 17:14 MSG

## DINO STATS

**FAMILY:**
Megalosauridae

**HEIGHT:**
Unknown

**LENGTH:**
22–30 ft.
(6.7–9.1 m)

**WEIGHT:**
1,500 lb.
(680.4 kg)

**DIET:**
meat

**DID YOU KNOW . . .** that the Dubreuillosaurus seemed to lack any crest or horns on its head?

# BROKEN BUT NOT DESTROYED

**DIGGING DEEPER:**

*Think of a time when someone hurt you. Has your heart healed from that hurt? If not, ask God, the healer of all healers, to help put you back together!*

**JURASSIC JOURNALING:**

*Write a letter to God about your worst heartbreak ever.*

Paleontologists haven't found enough fossils of the Dubreuillosaurus to reconstruct this giant dinosaur, but one thing is for sure—it had a huge head! Scientists say its head was three times as long as it was high. Discovered in 1994 inside a French quarry that was no longer used, the strange skull and a few ribs made scientists think it was a new species. However, by the time researchers returned to the quarry to recover more fossils, the quarry was back in use!

Unfortunately, the onsite bulldozers had smashed the remaining fossils into thousands of tiny pieces. It took scientists several years to collect all the pieces! In the end, they determined it was a Megalosaur and named it *Dubreuillosaurus Valesdunensis* after the Dubreuil family, who made the original discovery.

Have you ever felt broken? The phrase "broken heart" describes how it feels to be hurt, upset, disappointed, and overlooked. When someone you love hurts you deeply, your heart can actually feel like it's breaking into thousands of pieces. And when that happens, it's easy to think your heart will never be normal again. But I have good news for you: God is the repairer of broken hearts. He can take a heart that is broken into as many pieces as those dinosaur fossils and make it stronger than before. All you have to do is ask Him and then trust Him to do it. It may not happen overnight, but it will happen. It's also good to talk to a parent, school counselor, or another trusted adult in your life to help heal your heart.

# SINORNITHOSAURUS
## [sine-OR-nith-oh-SORE-us]

**BIBLE EXCAVATION:**

Words kill, words give life; they're either poison or fruit—you choose.

—PROVERBS 18:21 MSG

## DINO STATS

**FAMILY:**
Dromaeosauridae

**HEIGHT:**
18 in. (0.5 m)

**LENGTH:**
3–4 ft. (0.9–1.2 m)

**WEIGHT:**
3.5–15 lb.
(1.6–6.8 kg)

**DIET:**
meat

## SAY IT, DON'T SPRAY IT!

While it's been proven the Dilophosaurus did not spit poison as some movies have portrayed, scientists believe they might have discovered a venom-spitting dino after all.

Some believe the Sinornithosaurus had special grooves in its fang-like teeth that connected to pockets in the jaw that could've been full of venom. But other scientists insist the fang-like teeth weren't fangs at all. They say those long teeth look that way because they were crushed and partially pushed out of the jaw during the fossilization process. Bottom line? No one knows for sure if there ever lived a venom-spitting dinosaur, so the debate will continue until more proof comes to light.

But we know this for sure—we can be venom-spitting dinosaurs from time to time. Okay, we don't

DID YOU KNOW . . . that the name
*Sinornithosaurus* means "Chinese bird-lizard"?

**DIGGING DEEPER:**

*Think of a time when you shot poisonous words at someone. Did you ever apologize for saying those hurtful words? If not, ask God and the person you hurt for forgiveness.*

**JURASSIC JOURNALING:**

*Write the names of five friends or family members. Then write one thing you appreciate about that person. Now share the nice comment you wrote with each person!*

*actually* spit poison, but our words act just like poison when we say hurtful things. That's why we need to choose our words carefully. Our words can either build somebody up or tear somebody down. Think about it: Have you ever had poisonous words shot at you? They may not have killed you, but they probably hurt your heart and maybe crushed your spirit. If you have trouble keeping control of your mouth, ask God to help you. And remember the old saying "Say it, don't spray it" whenever you feel like being mean to someone. Say something kind or constructive, but keep that venom to yourself.

# MEI LONG
## [may LAWNG]

## DINO STATS

**FAMILY:**
Troodontidae

**HEIGHT:**
1–2 ft. (0.3–0.6 m)

**LENGTH:**
2–4 ft. (0.6–1.2 m)

**WEIGHT:**
8 lb. (3.6 kg)

**DIET:**
meat

# SWEET SLEEP

This little dinosaur was about the size of a large duck and had big nostrils, tons of teeth, and a small head. The Mei Long fossil was the first one to be discovered in a birdlike sleeping position—with its face tucked behind one wing-like claw. Some scientists think this dino may have been warm-blooded and would get in this position to stay warm so it could sleep through the night.

Speaking of sleep, do you get enough? Or do you make lots of excuses so you won't have to go to bed? Our bodies need sleep to function properly. Getting enough sleep improves your memory, boosts your immune system, sparks creativity, increases your athletic performance, improves your grades, helps you keep a healthy weight, lowers your stress, and so much more! Plus, it's important to honor your parents' wishes if they've given you a specific bedtime.

If you have trouble going to sleep, experts suggest taking a warm shower before bed, as well as wearing warm socks to bed. And you can ask God to help you fall asleep and stay asleep. Try praying right before you fall asleep. That's a great way to end the day and enter into sweet dreams.

**DIGGING DEEPER:**

*Do you have trouble falling asleep? If so, why? Have you tried praying right before you go to bed?*

**JURASSIC JOURNALING:**

*Make a list of things you can be thankful for, and instead of counting sheep, count your blessings as you try to fall asleep.*

**DID YOU KNOW . . .** that the name *Mei Long* means "soundly sleeping dragon"?

# ZUNICERATOPS
## [ZOO-nee-SERR-a-tops]

**BIBLE EXCAVATION:**

"Let the little children come to me, and do not hinder them, for the kingdom of God belongs to such as these. Truly I tell you, anyone who will not receive the kingdom of God like a little child will never enter it." And he took the children in his arms, placed his hands on them and blessed them.

—MARK 10:14–16 NIV

## YOU'RE NOT TOO YOUNG

**DINO STATS**

**FAMILY:**
Ceratopsidae

**HEIGHT:**
3–5 ft. (0.9–1.5 m)

**LENGTH:**
10–11 ft. (3–3.4 m)

**WEIGHT:**
220–330 lb.
(99.8–149.7 kg)

**DIET:**
plants

Some paleontologists go their whole lives without making an important discovery. But sometimes a person gets lucky and has a life-changing find at age eight! That's what happened to Christopher James Wolfe, the son of paleontologist Douglas G. Wolfe, in 1998 in New Mexico. His discovery was a big deal because the skull and bones he found turned out to be the earliest Ceratopsian to have horns over its eyes.

Can you imagine being eight years old and discovering an important dinosaur fossil? Pretty cool, huh? Well, God has great things ahead for you too. God loves to use young people to do amazing things! You see, He doesn't look at your age when determining your assignments. He looks at your faith. He looks at your heart. If you are willing to follow God, He will use you to do important things. You might be little, but you can have big faith and make a big impact on this world!

Do you know the story in John 6 about the little boy with five loaves and two fish? The boy thought he was just

*Have you ever wondered if God can use you? What are some ways you think He could use you even now, before you're an adult?*

## JURASSIC JOURNALING:

*Write down some examples of kids who have done amazing things. Maybe some of your friends are doing great things for God. It's important to remind yourself that you're not too young to be used by God.*

bringing his lunch along that day, but Jesus performed a miracle and used the food to feed more than five thousand people—all because the boy was willing to share. God can use you too, if you're willing. Your age doesn't matter; only your faith in God matters. He will make sure you're in the right place at the right time to do the right thing. Who knows? Maybe you'll be the next kid to help feed a crowd of hungry people or discover a dinosaur fossil.

**DID YOU KNOW** . . . that the horns of a Zuniceratops continued to grow throughout its life?

# TORVOSAURUS
## [TOR-voh-SORE-us]

**BIBLE EXCAVATION:**

"You have heard that it was said, 'Love your neighbor and hate your enemy.'
But I tell you, love your enemies and pray for those who persecute you."

—MATTHEW 5:43–44 NIV

## NOBODY LIKES A BULLY

### DINO STATS

**FAMILY:**
Megalosauridae

**HEIGHT:**
6–12 ft. (1.8–3.7 m)

**LENGTH:**
30–40 ft.
(9.1–12.2 m)

**WEIGHT:**
6,000–12,500
lb. (2,721.6–
5,669.9 kg)

**DIET:**
meat

**P**aleontologists agree that the Torvosaurus was a big, bad beast.

Because of its enormous size, this dinosaur was thought to be somewhat of a bully. In fact, researchers believe it may have used its larger size to steal food from smaller meat-eating dinosaurs such as the Marshosaurus, the Ceratosaurus, and even the Allosaurus! I'm guessing the Torvosaurus wasn't too popular. Nobody likes a bully.

Ever encountered a bully? Has anyone ever taken your lunch money, shoved you into a locker, or told lies about you? Of course, bullies don't have to be big to be bad. With the technology we have today, bullies of any size can leave hurtful comments about their victims all over social media. No matter how they hurt people, bullies can ruin people's lives. But you don't have to let them ruin yours.

We may not be able to stop the bullies from acting the way they do—although you should report any

**DIGGING DEEPER:**

*Have you ever been bullied? If you're being bullied right now, you need to tell someone you trust—your parents, a teacher, a school counselor, your pastor, or some other adult you're close to.*

**JURASSIC JOURNALING:**

*Write about a time when you were bullied. Share how it made you feel and how it changed you.*

bullying to a trusted adult—but we can change how we respond. Resist the urge to get back at the bully. The Bible says we shouldn't take revenge. Instead, we're supposed to let God handle it. He will! And keep your heart right in all of it. Do what the Bible says and pray for your enemies. It will keep your heart right and open the door for God to work in the heart of that bully. He loves bullies too.

**DID YOU KNOW** . . . that the name *Torvosaurus* means "savage lizard"?

# EOLAMBIA
## [EE-oh-LAM-bee-ah]

BIBLE EXCAVATION:

"Those who drink the water I give will never be thirsty again. It becomes a fresh, bubbling spring within them, giving them eternal life."

—JOHN 4:14 NLT

## GOT WATER?

**DINO STATS**

**FAMILY:**
Hadrosauroidea

**HEIGHT:**
6–7 ft. (1.8–2.1 m)

**LENGTH:**
20–30 ft.
(6.1–9.1 m)

**WEIGHT:**
2,200 lb. (997.9 kg)

**DIET:**
plants

The earliest-known duckbill, the Eolambia, is one of the more common dinosaurs. It had spikes on its thumbs, which experts believe it used to cut leaves off trees or possibly cut bigger plants into bite-size treats.

Since this dinosaur lived in a warm, dry world, scientists think it found nearby water sources to drink from, and it would munch on the major plant growth near the water. While it could've found plants to eat in other areas, it needed water to survive, so the dino found an all-you-can-eat-and-drink buffet—water and plants all in one area.

We also need water to survive—both physically and spiritually. Our bodies need water to energize our muscles, flush out toxins, prevent disease, and so much more. And our spirit needs the Living Water, which Jesus talks about in John 7:37: "Let anyone who is thirsty come to me and drink" (NIV). All Christians have the Living Water, which is the Holy Spirit, who teaches us God's will and guides us. When we ask Jesus to be

DIGGING DEEPER:

If you haven't asked Jesus to be the Lord over your life, you can do that right now by simply praying, "God, I know I've sinned, and I am sorry for what I've done wrong. I ask that You forgive me. I want You to be the Lord of my life from this moment forward. Amen."

JURASSIC JOURNALING:

If you just prayed that prayer, write the date in your journal and write, "Spiritual Birthday" next to it. Your new life starts today!

the Lord over our lives, the Holy Spirit comes to live in our hearts. It's the best thing that can ever happen to any of us! By making Jesus Lord over your life, you're not only guaranteed to live forever with Him in heaven one day, but He will also help you live a better life while here on earth.

Say yes to Jesus. Say yes to Living Water. Drink up!

DID YOU KNOW . . . that paleontologist James Kirkland named the Eolambia, as well as the Utahraptor and the Gastonia?

# SOURCES

activewild.com

a-dinosaur-a-day.com

ageofdinosaurs.com

animals.howstuffworks.com

Baker, Robert. *The Complete Guide to Dinosaurs* (New York: Sandy Creek Publishing, 2015)

bbc.com

Benton, Michael. *The Kingfisher Dinosaur Encyclopedia* (New York: Kingfisher, 2017)

blog.everythingdinosaur.co.uk

blogs.scientificamerican.com

britannica.com

Brown, David. "The Dinosaur That Peacefully Grazed," *Washington Post.* November 16, 2007. washingtonpost.com

cbc.ca

christianitytoday.com

Colson, Rob. *Dinosaur Bones: And What They Tell Us* (Richmond Hill: Firefly Books, 2016)

dailymail.co.uk

dinochecker.com

dinodictionary.com

dinopit.com

dinosaurfact.net

dinosaurhome.com

dinosaurjungle.com

dinosaurpictures.org

*Dinosaurs Eye to Eye* (London: Dorling Kindersley, 2010)

dinosaur-world.com

discovermagazine.com

Dixon, Dougal. *Amazing Dinosaurs: The Fiercest, the Tallest, the Toughest, the Smallest* (Honesdale: Boyds Mills Press, 2000)

dkfindout.com

drexel.edu

easyscienceforkids.com

enchantedlearning.com

famousscientists.org

health.com

Holtz, Thomas R. *Dinosaurs: The Most Complete, Up-to-Date Encyclopedia for Dinosaur Lovers of All Ages* (New York: Random House Books for Young Readers, 2007)

Kelly, Miles. *Encyclopedia of Dinosaurs and Prehistoric Life* (Thaxted: Miles Kelly Publishing, Ltd, 2017)

kidsdinos.com

kids-dinosaurs.com

kids.kiddle.co

kids.nationalgeographic.com

Lambert, David, Darren Naish, and Elizabeth Wyse, eds. *Encyclopedia of Dinosaurs & Prehistoric Life* (London: Dorling Kindersley, 2003)

Lessem, Don. *National Geographic Kids Ultimate Dino-Pedia, Second Edition* (Washington, DC: National Geographic, 2017)

livescience.com

McCall, Gerrie. *Dinosaurs: 300 Prehistoric Creatures*, revised ed. (London: Amber Books, 2016)

mentalfloss.com

nature.com

nbcnews.com

newdinosaurs.com

news.nationalgeographic.com

nhm.ac.uk

nhmu.utah.edu

phenomena.nationalgeographic.com

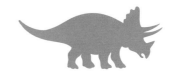

Pim, Keiron. *Dinosaurs: The Grand Tour* (New York: The Experiment, LLC, 2013)

prehistoric-wildlife.com

prehlife.weebly.com

rareresource.com

reuters.com

revolvy.com

sciencedaily.com

scienceviews.com

scified.com

sci-news.com

smithsonianmag.com

therecord.com

theregister.co.uk

thoughtco.com

ucmp.berkeley.edu

unmuseum.org